Struggle

Ministries

Turning Life Struggles into a Ministry for God

Table of Contents

Part One: Family of Origin

Chapter One Realization

"The only way to change your mind is to go to a deeper level of understanding where the experience becomes irrelevant."

-Deepak Chopra

IT WAS ME ALL ALONG MESSING UP MY LIFE! I chose the wrong people to share my life with. I put my trust in the wrong people. I was hearing God's Word constantly. Yet, I kept looking for the good in the people who wanted to ruin my life. Me, playing nice with the enemy, who I was supposed to be in battle with.

At an early age, I learned about Christ. I'm not talking about just a Jesus loves me faith, even though we will make it back to that. I was in love with the building, the Word, and the music. The way the ground shook when we were still in our original church building with creaky floors and limited heat. In love with the act of serving our Lord and others.

Also, How the Word of God seemed to bridge across generations to make things work out that couldn't without faith. I was filled with many questions so young. Some that could be answered by my elders. Others not so much. I unlike most children looked forward to Sunday school and each service. I was proudly summarizing the culmination of what we learned. I felt in my element assisting the elderly, ushering with sore feet, and trying to soak up as much as I could. My earliest memory is being as young as five or six trying to stay up during the sermon. No matter how hard I tried I was always met with the opened doors (call to accept Christ) of the church with the choir swaying and waving their hand.

Now in my 30s, I am learning the depth of Christ's love for me at a deeper level. I knew the stories. I read, studied, worshipped, and served 22 of those years. The thirst has been there always to learn more. I found my application and was satisfied with myself. I didn't know how much I was missing out on. The richness that flowed through the words of the Bible, OUTSIDE OF THE APPLICATIONS!

This journey for me up until this point I knew I was ill equipped, born damaged, approval seeking, and serving alone beyond my means. That resulted in me causing more damage to myself, to others, and ending up completely lost wondering how I arrived here starving and thirsty for life. I was longing for a life outside of the one I was currently living. "If I just make it out things will be different." That's what I told myself but, I've moved various places with the same result. A life of misery. A cup almost bare. Dragging myself to every obligation I signed up for because that's what we were supposed to do right? Make our family proud. Being successful. Get rich. Find a spouse. Have kids. All the milestones of life. There is so much goodness we are missing there. Myself seeking those life goals set in motion the hamster wheel of striving. Without knowing what these "accomplishments entail" we seek to find them with all our might.

Make our Family Proud and Succeed

The goal is ingrained into us from birth. Your parent(s) cheer when you smile at them. Have your first word, step, or learn something new. Approval and recognition feel good, so it becomes a habit of our lives to continue to seek for it and have it duplicated again and again. Not anything to look down on yourself about. We want our kids to be able to progress, learn, and grow. Did God create us for the purpose of pleasing our parents? Hmmmm. That would have a varying definition of accomplishments.

While as children, our expectations are normally laid out for us. As adults, expectations tend to be nonverbal. Due to most of us living with our parents around 18 years, they tend to assume we now know what the expectation is from them. I would say since 95% of that time was in school, we follow that track out first and see where it takes us then find a job and apply that work ethic again. They should be satisfied right? I find the relationship between parent and child continuously interesting because of how many metamorphoses could arise from two parents. Add divorce, moves, stepparents, job changes, and 1,000,000 other variables. The end goal most tend to end up with is to be the best and succeed. Even those not geared towards academics. Music or sports participators want to be the best and succeed at what they do. I have experienced many parents: of friends, elders in the church, and coworkers parents who actually say although success is the implied expectation. What they want is for their child(ren) to be happy. Interesting huh? As the kid, if you asked, "What would make your parents happy pertaining to your life?" The response probably wouldn't be "for me to live my life happy." If my purpose is to succeed for my parents and my parents' purpose is to succeed for their parents. So on and so forth. Who is actually living out their purpose or whose purpose of success are we fulfilling? People we've never met that are deceased but, the family continued some sense of their values or what they deemed important.

This applies to God too. Does he want us to succeed or be happy? What is our purpose?

Riches

This life goal ties into being successful but is a little different. This may be the product of the success. Money, albeit opens another can of worms. Why do we want to be rich? What do we want to use the money for? We hear repeatedly from celebrities that money and being rich isn't all it's cracked up to be. Larger empires require more people to be managed, more people to pay, and larger problems to repair.

That thought affected my, day to day thought just this week. I was working on my poetry book "Fall Back" which I decided to fully self publish myself. I was frustrated with the formatting, to say the least. I was thinking:

"What if I can't figure this out?"

"I can't pay someone to do the formatting because my car is in the shop."

"I'm about to leave for a spring break trip for Virginia. I need to hurry."

I wanted to have money available in case something went wrong with our flight. I was at my wits end and after hours of trying to figure this out. It hit me, if everyone on this earth has the same 24 hours as me, I should be grateful. Grateful that this isn't something like a concert, that thousands of people had paid money for with me considering cancelling the show. I was thinking about how many times, I just don't feel like it today. The rich become paid workers. They have management. Who majority of the time abandons the role of helping the artist, into getting as much work booked in to every 24 hours. Most celebrities don't feel like they have the authority to set that relationship back in order. They are being dragged around from event to event exhausted. Most just wanting to go back home to their kids or rest. Also, the more you buy the more maintenance. A larger home comes with a larger property tax. As they say in the culture, "more money, more problems." Think of the guilt you would feel calling out for a sick day or for wanting to spend time with your family. Is this a healthy goal for us to be chasing?

Find a Spouse and have Kids

Wheeeeew! This one has been the hardest for me to process. The majority of my life has been about being in a relationship. It was not until after many years of therapy did I realize how big a deal it was to bring others into your space. I want you to consider your life being a big ball of yarn. All in a tangled mess. Some strings are things you understand. Other strings are filled with confusion tying knots around the ones you understand. Then, some partially understood and some even broken (frayed edged) or cut (sharp edged). Therapy began to help me pull those strings out one at a time and began to help me understand them. Just learning about yourself and trying to figure out life. A person deciding to add a new relationship into that dynamic while still untangling would be difficult. It doesn't keep you from longing for someone but, it does cause you to consider what you may be seeking in that relationship. Is it comfort? Is it protection?

Kids are similar EXCEPT they can't manage themselves. Babies have to have everything done for them. Toddlers have tantrums and need things repeatedly explained to them. Then as that child has milestones or challenges you have to help them untangle their small balls of yarn while constantly spilling a little of your tangles onto them. You can see how starting a family complicates things greatly. This book is about you though. Not these things we as a society consider success.

Our scales are removed from our eyes when God allows. Now that I can see, I have no idea how I could see it any other way. Yet I did! Now I have to go back and hold myself accountable. But guess what? While taking accountability, I will bring others with me. Our eyes are covered by scales not because He doesn't love us but the opposite. God does love us. How can we relate to each other better than walking the same path? Yes, I know you are thinking it. No two lives are identical. So true, but aren't there shared experiences? The details won't be the same but, the lesson is. When we finally learn that lesson, is up to God. What do we get to do for others before the scales are removed? We get to love them through their journey. What a great call to only have to love others as Christ loves us. Not that we can or have to do it perfectly. God says our best is enough:

"Owe no one anything, except to love each other, for the one who loves another has fulfilled the law." Romans 13:8 ESV[1]

Christ has already come down and loved us perfectly.

---

[1] https://bible.com/bible/59/rom.13.8.ESV

"For the love of Christ controls us, because we have concluded this: that one has died for all, therefore all have died;" 2 Corinthians 5:14 ESV[2]

During the process of sanctification[3], defined by Merriam-Webster as "the act of freeing from sin or moral guilt," we die to our flesh repeatedly to be obedient to God doing as He tells us. More plainly put we give up our wants for what God wants. I may want to stay home on Sundays and sleep. God calls us to be in His place of worship and fellowshipping with other believers.

We get to tell the next person, although I have not lived your life or walked in your shoes, I made it out of a sin struggle. So can you! I will hold your hand while you do it and I will love you through it. Backsliding and all. We aren't called to expect perfection from each other but, to constantly forgive. Forgiveness is apart of the action of love.

"Be kind to one another, tender-hearted, forgiving one another, as God in Christ gave you." Ephesians 4:32 ESV[4]

---

[2] https://bible.com/bible/59/2co.5.14.ESV

[3] https://www.merriam-webster.com/dictionary/sanctification

[4] https://bible.com/bible/59/eph.4.32.ESV

If I was a man, it would be hard for me to share an experience about a woman. If I was childless, it would be hard for me to advise a mother on parenting. Yet, Christ gives us the full body of the church. Each of us bringing if nothing else to the table except life experience. That is enough to save lives. God can work with those who are willing and able to be shaped by His potter hands. All He needs is your yes!

Something I've been convicted to learn more about even now is the words "in Christ." Even here in Ephesians, I'm awakened to something I haven't paid much attention to even after reading it hundreds if not thousands of times. God is FORGIVING US IN CHRIST. Yes, we think of it as because of Christ but "In Christ" hits my heart, my spirit different today. We can only love others through their hardships and pain "in Christ." He already knows if left to our own strengths we couldn't do it. That's why Christ was sent.

Chapter Two Family Shortcomings

Let me start off by saying, I am not attacking any of my family members. I love them. I'm working towards loving the harder ones exactly as they are. These are my observations from my personal, individualized, unique walk in my family. I am glad to now be a part of God's family as His true fully loved daughter. It makes me then appreciate my family as they are because my expectations are lowered. Once again unspoken expectations, I know from studying that God handpicked every single one of the people who I've encountered, touched, and will meet in my life and their individual role. If one person or interaction was removed something about me would be different. I may be less compassionate in an area or less driven at work. We don't know what the change would be, and we shouldn't want to know. God placed you in this time period to uncover His glory to others.

> "For I know the plans I have for you, declares the Lord, plans for welfare and not for evil, to

give you a future and a hope." Jeremiah 29:11ESV[5]

Every single conversation helped to form how you think. It shaped and molded the way you speak to people. One thing I can say truly that I love about my family of origin is the way they approach a stranger or someone in need. They barely blink an eye before they jump in to start helping, start feeding, clothing, or invite people to fellowship. Jesus was all about seeking more people to fellowship with. We learn through experiences with others. To soften the day, week, or years of someone's life for just a little while doing God's work. We can help show the hope that we can have in Jesus.

As a black adult woman, I don't feel as if I can have the conversation with my mother or grandmother about things I went through with them. In my family, you don't fully get to be an adult until you are the actual elder. There is always judgment or someone to say something about your every move unless you go off and do your own thing. You are always seen as a kid. That alone puts us behind in society. At age 18, most Caucasians are seen as adults. This allows the to mature into an adult a lot quicker and develop emotionally. If you would have

[5] https://bible.com/bible/59/jer.29.11.ESV

asked me two years ago what I felt my emotional maturity[6] age is, I would probably say somewhere between 10-14. Five years ago, when I had my daughter probably an eight. Today maybe 24.

I was 24 when I had my daughter. I was married at 28. Divorced at 28. It was not until I began to do real therapy. Not how was your day therapy, did I begin to see my immaturity for myself. I realize now today my mom was depressed for the majority of my life. I don't know if she knew that. What I do know is how I felt during this time. Alone. I knew, it was said often, my mother never wanted to have kids. She ended up with two at age 21. Although, she was my mom I didn't know much about her. I knew she wanted to be a model. She loved Michael Jackson and Michael Jordan. I couldn't tell you much more than that. She didn't go to college until I was in elementary school and middle school. She was always busy, working, and socializing. Not sure if these were apart of a plan. I only knew I had a lot of time on my hands. My grandparents had no cable, didn't let us watch TV over an hour, and made us go outside a lot. I wrote in my diary a lot about boys and

---

[6] Dr. Lindsay C. Gibson defines emotional maturity as "people who are capable of taking a look at themselves and reflecting on their (own) behavior." Gibson, Lindsay C. *Adult Children of Emotionally Immature Parents*. Oakland, New Harbinger, 2015.

boys only. Friends were the occasional topic. My mom, brother, and stepdad popped up as a topic on bad days. The only hope I had was the next boyfriend and whatever new thing that was coming up at school. My number one hope was to be 18 and move far away. It couldn't come fast enough.

I was raised in the south surrounded by strong women. I was mostly around my grandmother's siblings. There were five girls and two boys. The two great uncles I have were married before I was born so I only knew aunts and uncles. Our family was so enmeshed I didn't know who was married in and who was a blood relative. An amazing aspect of our family that I would say is admirable. It was engrained in me that whoever I ended up with would be involved in this family. I could talk forever about each of them but for the sake of time I will use a grouping of two.

Career vs. Homemaker

The homemakers are the majority in my family. They married young and didn't work much out of the home. They were top-notch nurturers. My mom never had to worry about childcare because they were always home. Never a problem for them to keep the kids. Great cooks, tons of outside play, endless soap operas, and naps. This was the place for exploration and a cousin's summer dream. One of my favorite things we did as kids every summer is that the five of us: three boys and two girls would spend one week at each aunt's home. We stayed as a group but experienced life in each place. Fun times but, again gelling together the idea of family working together to serve the family. The tendency of these women though was proper church attendance and a ton of focus on housework. The boys mostly played outside, while the girls dusted, washed dishes, and helped to cook. The boys' chores seemed minimal. There was no fun for us until the chores were done. The husbands of this group of women were always out doing stuff. They were working or running some errands, but rarely home.

Camp number two were the career women. Now these women were on the move. Always at work eight to five if not longer. Sometimes on and off working on higher education. They still took off that week in the summer to spend with family. I have only considered one a workaholic. This woman also vacations as much as she works. One thing about these women though is that they were the ones that were easier to relate to. They were the aunts you would want to ask for dating advice. The career women were younger and also used more energy dating. Not hard to find a mate but, hard to select correctly. As a kid it seemed to be two extremes but, the constant between the two camps were family, faith, image, and education.

Education and Image

Education was beat into my and my cousin's heads constantly right next to the Bible. My great grandfather was a sharecropper.[7] Definitely a larger part of the influence towards the family. My grandmother's siblings all were highly intelligent. Salutatorians. Valedictorians. Only three went to college, I think. There was always the expectation of exceptional grades and we kids produced. Not all of us through went to college that disrupted elements of our family at large.

It's the clash of the generations. If you don't accept my way, then I will disengage from the family. The older generation sees it as love and, "I'm trying to help you by steering you on the right path." The younger generation being pressed on feeling the pressure of expectations that were repeated verbally often. Then there is me in the middle enduring the

---

[7] "a tenant farmer especially in the southern U.S. who is provided with credit for seed, tools, living quarters, and food, who works the land, and who receives an agreed share of the value of the crop minus charges" https://www.merriam-webster.com/dictionary/sharecropper

older generation criticisms while conversing with the younger generation. The biggest issue I saw was a lack of honesty and transparency. The older generation acted as if they had never made mistakes. Also, they kept secrets to where if they did make a mistake it wasn't learned by the family. Even so, they never talked to a person from a place of empathy and compassion. The younger generation is so hurt that they no longer want to engage in toxic behavior anymore because, they have already dealt with it their whole lives.

There are no true relationships being formed here, only superficial ones. What it took for me to realize this began with an idea I had that stemmed from church. There was an idea to get to know other members of the church better to engage them with this list of 25 questions. These questions started vague, progressing into more personal questions. On top of completing it for church, I decided to send it to all my family members that I had an email for. Although we didn't make it through the entire list of questions, I do feel it opened a window for our relationship to where they knew someone in their family just wanted to get to know them for who they are. Isn't that what we all want? Just to be seen. This caused me to visit my family alone so I could talk to them one on one and not in a group. That began my evolution with my older generation.

The Big Three

The three most important people in my life as a kid was my grandmother, my mom, and Aunt Alice. Let's start with the easiest first. My Aunt Alice was always dear to me because I spent a ton of time with her. When my grandparents had a doctor's appointment we would stay with her. I would help her a lot because she had physical issues. On Sunday, my job would be to help her around. In that we bonded and could talk about anything. I think she was the first person to talk to me about sex. She asked me if I was pregnant one time because I got sleepy when I got off the bus due to my period starting. I was in like the fifth grade. Now that I think about it, that was possible but whoa! I probably admired her honesty. Sadly, she passed away while I was in high school leaving a hole of guidance to be missed.

Secondly, my grandmother. That amazingly wonderful woman. Our first encounters were very painful because we would argue about my clothes starting around middle school. One day I overheard my mom and grandmother arguing. I saw my grandmother cry. I knew us arguing before made her cry, so I never went at it like that with her again. From that moment on, my grandmother was and is my best friend. I talk to her constantly. I stopped playing with my brother and stayed inside to baked with her. We colored together, sewed, and completed word searches. Sometimes an attempt at a puzzle or two and lots of serving others. My grandmother was apart of that homemaker crew that beat us over the head about always going to church and what to wear. Nitpicking what I have on when I show up to her house. The list of things I'm doing wrong that should be fixed. I wasn't special in receiving this feedback. All of my cousins got it. I was just the one that stayed in the midst of my rebellion and said I still know you love me. I kept the good and discarded myself of the bad.

Third, but not least my mother. Me saying this was a troubled relationship would be an understatement but not from a lack of love. A ton of lack of everything else. There wasn't much arguing as it was with my grandmother. It was more of what was not being done, not feeling seen, and not being empathized with. I never felt more alone than when I was home with my mom and brother. We've had stepdads in and out but, outside of that it was the three of us. My mom worked a lot, so we were dragged along with her. Included in these hours were weekends, long nights, and events. When she wasn't at work, she was always doing something. Events for her sorority, keeping nieces and nephews, or more schoolwork. After she found a steady job, she still didn't stay within the hours of eight to five. We stayed in activities and sports. My brother was in piano, baseball, basketball, football, tennis, swimming, and golf. I did the exact same thing excluding football and adding in some STEM[8] and lots of reading.

It was like we explored everything until we found what we liked. The theme that sticks out though was, the separation between parent and child. We stayed with our grandmother a lot of my childhood. We slept there during the week and saw our mom on the weekends during a period. Sometimes she had things to do on the weekend, so we didn't see her then either. She also had a very colorful dating life that I felt pushed us down on the totem pole. Until recently, I thought this characterized my entire life but, now I see it was mostly my teens I felt the most alone, around middle school and high school. During this vital time, I was discovering boys, drama, the internet, and texting.

---

[8] Stem-science, technology, engineering, and mathematics

Many of these things I needed direction in. I talked to my mom about parts of my life but, I just didn't feel she was interested in who I was as a person. Have you ever talked to someone and they said "uh huh, uh huh, uh huh." Unconsciously, I knew what engaging conversation was because I remember how I felt when I talked to my aunt.

I had many expectations when it came to my mom. I would say my expectations for her would probably have resided somewhere near to where the top of the tower of Babel may have been. I see now some of it was unfair to ask of her. Only now at 30 can I see that my mom was severely depressed and doing a lot more than she should have been. She still has things on her plate she has been trying to get off for 10+ years. I'm just learning to take things off my plate myself. I wanted a mom who was a mix between a stay-at-home mom and a working mom. The mother God gave me was a working mother, a people serving mother, and a late education seeking mother. In the midst of two crazily opposite kids going through school and a couple of marriages. It's a blessing all of us are alive and mentally well.

My grandmother was a great example of active listening[9]. She was asking me questions and looking forward to seeing me. Even as a child, you can tell when someone wants you around or not. For my mom, I would try hard to have everything done when she arrived home so she wouldn't have an excuse to not be engaged: bathrooms cleaned, rooms swept and vacuumed, dishes and clothes washed, and food cooked. Food was a particularly sore point for me because I would be so bored during the summers. I would explore recipes for my family and I to try. I would time for it to be ready for the exact time she would arrive home. Much to my disappointment she would sit in the car for 30 minutes to an hour while I stood in the doorway pacing and waiting. Then she would come in, speak lightly, then go to her room and shut the door. The start to the loneliest years of my life.

---

[9] Active listening is defined as "a communication technique used in counselling, training and conflict resolution, which re- quires the listener to feed back what they hear to the speaker, by way of re-stating or paraphrasing what they have heard in their own words, to confirm what they have heard and moreover, to confirm the understanding of both parties." Sajid, Noor. *Hearing Research Journal: Active Listening*. United Kingdom, Elsevier BV, 2021.

My father had a similar dissociation[10] as my mother. He had been married a good number of years but, rarely stayed home. He would pick me up maybe one weekend out of the month and drop me off at my grandmother's then pop back up to take me home. As I grew older, I would get picked up by him and taken to his home with my bonus mom and my brothers. We would do stuff together then he would bring me home. Outside of that, I ran into him often on the church circuit because he was a singer and performed a lot of solos. He served in the military and is an exceptionally functional alcoholic. Of course, we rarely hold men accountable (me included). We just say, "he doesn't know any better." Also, I'm a girl and he's a guy. What is the conversation supposed to be like between a father and a daughter?

Things I Gained from my Family of Origin

1. My Connection to Christ

My deepest connection to Christ started with singing. I was falling in love with the sway, the stomp, the rocking of the church. It kept me focused at an

---

[10] Dissociation: to separate from association or union with another https://www.merriam-webster.com/dictionary/dissociate

age when it was hard to stay awake for an entire sermon. I remember getting mad at myself for waking up at the end of the sermon knowing I missed the entire messages from that day. Then, around ten I began note-taking and never stopped.

2. Commitment to Prayer

Now prayer was always a part of my daily life. We were taught to say prayers before we ate. Prayers every night. Now most of my prayers were me asking to be delivered from my hell home via rapture or peaceful death. I thought to myself I must be adopted or was swapped at birth. I prayed over my test starting in middle school maybe even before. It wasn't until maybe when my uncle died in 2005 that I started praying for day-to-day things.

It was July 25, 2005 on my mom's birthday when the phone rang.

"Hello."

"Can I speak to your mom?"

"One second."

She was in the bathroom.

I handed her the phone and turned to return to my room.

3 seconds later. . .

Blood curdling screams I've never heard before. At this time, I was in middle school and still pretty innocent. Innocent meaning not knowing much about the bad of the world. This would be the first taste of knowing what the place I have been sent to bear is. . .

. . . My eldest uncle had been killed by a roadside bomb (IED-Improvised Explosive Device) in Baghdad, Iraq.

I remembered that scream went on for what seemed like an eternity. The door to the bathroom was locked so all I could do was sit by the door until she opened it. I did exactly that and took care of her from that point on. This is the first time I consciously pushed my feelings out of the way for the feelings of someone else. The next emotion I remember is being sad for my grandfather. This was not my grandmother's child but had been around him for many years by this point and had grown fond of him. He was extremely hard not to love with his flashy pearly whites and infectious laughter. We made it back home to my grandfather before the military arrived to deliver that folded flag.

I remember parts of the funeral vividly and other parts not so much. I remember being upset because I couldn't see him to say goodbye. Feels weird to say to not tell a middle schooler a means of death. Although, in this particular instance I wish I didn't know. I could only think about the pieces of him inside that casket or even that they had all of this wrong. They identified the wrong man. He is going to walk right in here and shock us all. That time though never came and only the laughing echoes remained.

The living heck was scared out of me. I had no idea what to do. My mom had locked herself in the bathroom screaming. I didn't yet know what was wrong or how to get in the bathroom. I had no idea who to call. That one phone call changed everything. We moved from a prosperous place for my mom's job, my stepdad's job, and school for me back to my dead-end hometown.

We moved back to a town where we were poor, schools were under challenging, and there was a lot more free time for trouble. I was stuck in the house with my brother who liked to have his way with no protection for me. More on that to come. I became held together by prayer at all times. Day to day, night to night, hour to hour, minute to minute, and second to second. As I prayed, I learned how to lean and depend on God. How can I lean on Him without knowing He's a rock? I learned how to stand on a foundation He built for me rock by rock. A rock holding each day of hardship that I had to endure that he brought me through. Could I fully depend on Him if I never had to rely on Him? Prayer is so underestimated even by myself until this day. I am very unsure of knowing how to ask for the things I need because I am afraid of my own intentions. God, though when I proclaim His will be done surrounding my need, He takes care of all the emotions that surrounds it. Prayer wasn't so hard to adapt to, but gratefulness truly was.

3. Don't Forget the Forgotten

Another piece that I learned from my family was to not forget the forgotten. My grandmother turned 80 this year. At this moment, she is in the hospital due to a bowel obstruction. (Yeah, I know. She would want me to be writing. It's okay.) For as long as I could remember the birthdays of all regular and irregular church members, every member of our family, in laws, classmates, & family friends: Not only does she remember them, she puts a card in the mail every year that is timed to perfection to arrive on their birthday. This doesn't include the cards she sends for losses in the family, celebrations, or births. This woman who I love never forgot until this year. Let's explore how that went.

When my grandmother was out of the hospital, she mentioned a few birthdays she forgot to send out cards for. I informed her that no one would be upset or disappointed. They knew she was in the hospital. People were calling constantly to check on her. I also said, "Grandma, you did it all of those years. No one could be angry to never receive one again." She had been doing this since I was born.

Note on Gratitude

This was around the time a popular daytime TV host started talking about gratitude journals. They were in every store, gift shop, and mom and pop shop. I would keep trying to do the practice but, it would be so mind numbing. I rolled my eyes when I tried. I couldn't get past food, shelter, water, things I needed for school, my body, mind, and soul. My creativity had been stifled for a while but, I didn't know why. Imagine someone who thought happiness was joy while trying to be thankful. It may make sense that I wouldn't know what to be thankful for when I wasn't making any real connections. Only surface level ones.

4. Faithfulness to the Mission

Something that has proved valuable to me is my family knows what it means to stay faithful and steadfast when it comes to staying true to the mission God has allowed us to take part in. I have learned to serve by watching my grandparents serve their church community, friends, and strangers, a countless number of times. Multiple people in my family decided to feed the elderly in their surrounding communities. You were very honored if any of them made a plate for you because they were comfort food master chefs. After every holiday, we would make plates for the people that were sick and shut in[11].

My grandfather always cut grass for older people who weren't able or of women who were unmarried. I never knew that until I was an adult. We would schedule a cemetery or church cleaning on Sunday for the following Saturday. My grandparents would pick a day during the week to take initiative and do it first, leaving the congregation with nothing

---

[11] Hospitals, nursing homes, jails, and people immobile from no car, injuries, surgeries, etc.

to do. My grandfather many times was the first person in the door and the last person to leave. We would visit the elderly or people who had no family even in an old two door Firebird Pontiac with no air. We took other people to church and to their doctor's appointments with or without room. My brother and I lived with my grandparents a good bit, occasionally with a visit from a cousin or two. The grandparents that always had a place to be, something to always do, but never in a rushed way. If we were home there was cleaning, yard work, and gardening to be done. For church, of course also work, more serving and praising to be done. Always a stop to be made to check on a neighbor when all we wanted to do was go home. How quick would we be to say, "I can't help with this or that thing because I am keeping my grandchild." This amazing man and woman of God knew that just meant they would have more hands, legs, and smiles available for the next task.

Chapter Three Envy the Boy

Being the first born, you are the one that is supposed to set the example for your siblings. I had three younger brothers. Two lived with my dad. One lived with me in the household with my mom. The one I shared a home with could have his way at any moment. What it would be to feel free and able to live life without thinking of consequences. I was so graciously given that conscience to not let down my mom, dad, church, grandparents, family, and whomever else I had imagined I could let down. I have never been able to do not even one thing without a voice saying this and that could happen. Millions of possibilities resulting from one decision none of them resulting in a positive result.

Social drinking was the only thing that quieted those lingering thoughts. Not in a good way. That's how I ended up with munchkin. When we were over 21, the one thing my brother and I usually enjoyed together was that. Not that we went to the club together but if we were around family. The groupings ended up being the young people doing their thing and the older crowd went their way. If you fall in the middle, you pick a side. Holidays are stressful for my family because someone is always calling you to do this or that. Not sure if we waited too late to have kids so we didn't have anyone else to call on to do anything. Us entering our 30s still doing the chores of little kids. The fact that the pattern repeats itself time after time doesn't help. The only thing that has improved is that we can drink. We still play games like we did as kids. Us being raised in a small town there is so little to do. Practically everyone is drinking at all times. In college, I only drank if it was a special weekend like homecoming or a club night. The bonding started and stopped there.

If only a couple of days to let my hair down and have the mind of my brother. No consequences, not getting caught by adults, or cops. Just hopping free as a bird from place to place. He lived life floating around in the wind. Steadily having someone to call if things went south. Jumping railroad tracks in a free and clear paid off car. Not caring if it didn't crank tomorrow. Go to a job, start, and free to quit at the drop of a hat. No worries about what's next or plans for the future. A life of my dreams. Possibly what my retirement would look like.

I'm sure I would have to read up on research but, I have a hunch that all siblings think that some other sibling has it better or easier than them. Also, when it comes to the debate of who's the favorite and most spoiled: parents would say it's equal.

Siblings would say it's the opposite sibling. Which is true? Your truth of course. Everyone's own experience is their truth because their world is life from their point of view, feelings, and thoughts. My brother and I have always had a painfully complicated relationship. We don't do half siblings in my family. We share a mom and were raised together. I was born from an unplanned pregnancy. My brother was born from a marriage a year and a half later. My mom divorced from his dad while we were at a young age. My mom went to college in her 30s. Due to that, we were at my grandparents a lot. My brother was a hyperactive child. He was always doing something, touching something, or getting into trouble.

Me on the other hand, the polar opposite. I was quiet. I could entertain myself for hours, still can. I would color, read, or write. Anytime my brother and I tried to do something together it meant a fight was bound to happen. We would play cards, wrestle, play basketball, and ride bikes. Fights would usually erupt from high emotions surrounding my brother wanting something that was mine or I was using. I would be enjoying myself and minding my business. For instance, I'm the one in the swing then he wants to be on the swing. He cheated in any game we played. It became pointless after a while. It wasn't enjoyable for me if we weren't going to play fair and be on equal footing. I think that started my relationships with the older crowd. I just did whatever the older folks did. Grandma was cooking. I helped her and let my brother play on his own with neighborhood cousins and friends. When I wasn't helping grandma, I was READING. Oh, how I loved to read. The joy of getting to read a book from the library then, return it for something new. Twice a week at minimum, I would go to the library for new books. The library played a vital role in my summers.

When we were in middle school around 2005, we moved into the city for six months. After a lifetime of country living, that started the room sharing. Oh my gosh, to this day I don't know how we survived that. I remember having posters of Bow Wow and B2K all over the walls and my desktop computer. When those six months were up, we moved to Georgia where we still shared a room. Except this time, we had a TV in our room. That's what the fighting ended up being about, what we would watch and when. This was during the time the living room TV was for adults. This was also the first time we had cable TV. It was an exciting time during the cartoon golden era 2000s. My brother usually wanted to watch the childlike boy cartoons. I was usually planning for the more mature movies and shows with a deeper meaning. In those days, you couldn't stream a show when you wanted to. You had to time it perfectly for the start of the movie to get to see it. Also, we tattled on each other constantly and someone was always on punishment. Around late elementary school and middle school, I did get in trouble a lot during this time but, only for attitude. We had a stepdad during this period that I did not get along with, we argued constantly. My punishment mostly involved no cell phone since I had recently received one around 13. Devastating to the social life of a middle schooler to have your phone taken away. The drama!

In high school, there was lots of arguing because I was blackmailed by my brother that he would tell our mom certain stuff if I didn't do XYZ. Normally, that involved whatever he wanted me to do, usually his chores. This started a continued uneven balance of power in our relationship. I wasn't the strongest or meanest sibling. I ended up doing my chores and his just to keep the peace. I spent majority of my time locked in my room. It was me trying to escape reality, quickly becoming a professional at it. I would try to stay over at anyone's house I could.

In my ninth grade year, I was invited to apply for a college level boarding school. This was the escape I had been waiting for and I didn't even know it. The light of happiness came on and stayed on a while for me. For him, I think it grew a hatred or resentment towards me. Not sure which yet. There were lots of arguments about how much money was spent for me to be at my residential school which started tenth grade because we had to pay tuition, but it was for books and food. Nothing like college tuition but around three to five thousand dollars a year. During the summer, though I had to be home; I hated every minute of it. I counted down the days until it was time for me to leave again every summer while I was on the bus leaving town. About a three-hour drive from home. I had $100 a month for my allowance to use for: my hair, feminine products, snacks, and body care. The biggest things we did for fun at school was to go to the movies or to the mall. That all involved spending money. It would come out of that allowance.

For college, I moved even further away to Louisiana which was a six-and-a-half-hour drive away from my home. I had arrived in freedom land. Far away enough from the influence of home and expectations of my family. There could be no one driving up to surprise me. My complicated relationship with my brother continued probably up until recently. By recently, I mean within the last two years. Partially, I contribute it to age. He is now 29, the lack of maturity drove me nuts. I was always very mature for my age. I attribute our relationship success to God's blessed creation of the increasingly improving mental health field.

What Growth has been Made

Without going into detail in this book, I was diagnosed with depression[12] and anxiety[13] possibly four to five years ago. In the last two, I was diagnosed with Post Traumatic Stress Disorder (PTSD[14]). I take medication for my mood, and it helps immensely. Without it, I am pretty angry and irritable. Newly

---

[12] " Mood disorder that is marked by varying degrees of sadness, despair, and loneliness and that is typically accompanied by inactivity, guilt, loss of concentration, social withdrawal, sleep disturbances, and sometimes suicidal tendencies" https://www.merriam-webster.com/dictionary/depression

[13] "An abnormal and overwhelming sense of apprehension and fear often marked by physical signs (such as tension, sweating, and increased pulse rate), by doubt concerning the reality and nature of the threat, and by self-doubt about one's capacity to cope with it" https://www.merriam-webster.com/dictionary/anxiety

[14] "Traumatic event, particularly an event that involves actual or threatened death or serious bodily injury to oneself or others and that creates intense feelings of fear, helplessness, or horror. The symptoms of post-traumatic stress disorder include the reexperiencing of the trauma either through upsetting thoughts or memories or, in extreme cases, through a flashback in which the trauma is relived at full emotional intensity." https://www.britannica.com/science/post-traumatic-stress-disorder

found out for me, close to irrational. There are things that have taken place on my brother's side and my own that have improved our relationship and cooled our temperaments. We now view each other more as comrades or battle buddies than siblings. The rivalry still pops up from time to time but leaps and bounds from the past. We completely avoided each other in certain points of our lives. He is still blocked from my social media page. Every time I unblock him there is some drama but, we still tag each other in posts and send messages through the site.

There are going to be people in your life that you have to keep at arms length. God tells us though to guard our hearts.

"Keep your heart with all vigilance, for from it flow the springs of life." Proverbs 4:23   ESV[15]

> "And the peace of God, which surpasses all understanding, will guard your hearts and your minds in Christ Jesus." Philippians 4:7 ESV[16]

I'll give you some reasons as to why he was to be envied the most in my life. Number one: he is the

---

[15] https://bible.com/bible/59/pro.4.23.ESV
[16] https://bible.com/bible/59/php.4.7.ESV

baby. There are so many perks to being the baby. Special attention in day-to-day life. Him having a tantrum means he gets to have his way. He gets constantly bailed out for plainly put, insane things. He is excused from disrespectful behavior because it's played off as joking. Boys have less pressure when it comes to performing academically. Guys get a lot more dating privileges than girls because they can't get pregnant. Also, I really was a golden child outside of the teenage attitude. He benefited from that greatly. If I was a lawless ingrate, it may have turned out differently. The biggest reason to envy him though is in our family there were only the three of us. Me, him, and mom. He and mom trumped me A LOT. What are we going to eat? Do today? What movie to watch? Etc. They seemed to always be on the same page. I was outvoted. At some point, I learned my opinions didn't matter.

As a result of beginning to slowly give up, I thought what was the point of pressing for what I wanted if I was going to lose every time? He had mom's ear, always and still does. Only writing this now I can see how I've been run over in relationships for my whole life. My preference never mattered there so I never added my input. If I didn't add my input, I couldn't lose. I always in relationships only focused on what the other person needed and wanted. Like a servant, coming to do chores, even some entertainment, and using my body like I was some kind of circus show always having to get a standing ovation.

Oh, to be free to do what I want in the moment is what I envied the most. To not care so much, to be able to rebel against things that angered me. Now though. Today. I love that I care as much as I do. I am starting to see my emotions and compassion as superpowers. Given by God. Being free from a romantic relationship has allowed me to know myself and my family better. Also, to release the expectations I have put on them and awaken them to their expectations of me, and that they should no longer anticipate that girl. I do feel reborn.

> "And have put on the new self, which is being renewed in knowledge after the image of its creator." Colossians 3:10 ESV[17]

> "Therefore, if anyone is in Christ, he is a new creation. The old has passed away; behold, the new has come." 2 Corinthians 5:17 ESV[18]

---

[17] https://bible.com/bible/59/col.3.10.ESV
[18] https://bible.com/bible/59/2co.5.17.ESV

"And to be renewed in the spirit of your minds," Ephesians 4:23 ESV[19]

> "For the law of the Spirit of life has set you free in Christ Jesus from the law of sin and death." Romans 8:2 ESV[20]

When we are in relationship with God it is a relationship of security. Your opinions, thoughts, and feelings matter here in God's kingdom. We are all His favorites, and all get all of His time. When you observe behaviors that are repeated, act accordingly. I'm not saying people can't change but, they have to want to change on their own. You are only responsible for your own actions and responses. If you notice someone brings out the worst in you, create that distance. If something isn't sitting right in your spirit about one's intentions listen to that and proceed with caution. Trust is to be earned.

---

[19] https://bible.com/bible/59/eph.4.23.ESV
[20] https://bible.com/bible/59/rom.8.2.ESV

Part Two: Fulfillment Failed

Chapter Four Running to Freedom

"The sudden disappointment of a hope leaves a scar which the ultimate fulfillment of that hope never entirely removes."

-Thomas Hardy[21]

All searches for freedom begin with the need for escape. My demand was for more than one reason. One, my family dynamic of being worthless outside of my academic achievements. Two, I needed safety and space from the people that abused me. Three, freedom to be 100% myself, a top priority for me. There were multiple things that kept those priority for me.

In order to fully understand, you need to know I have lived with depression since the age of

---

[21] Hardy, Thomas and Millgate, Michael. The Life and Work of Thomas Hardy. United Kingdom, Palgrave Macmillan UK,1984.

13, happiness has always been hard for me. Various times in my life I tried to remember back to a time when I was happy. The first time I can recall is being in elementary school coming home everyday excited to share what I learned. I was happy to see my friends every day. My friends were happy to see me everyday. Me loving to learn new things. I felt the darkness creeping in around middle school. I didn't know if it was because of puberty or life circumstances. That's a huge question for me. Let's explore a little of both. Puberty: all I remember was that I was already what they used to call "boy crazy." My focus in middle school shifted from 10% of my day being about boys to 98%. That's when you start "passing notes." Do they do that anymore? Love notes, stuffing notes in lockers, planning times to run into people to get our message along. With that came the drama of peering noses and gossip.

Middle school seemed to be the place where a lot of things begin to converge. The newness of being around a different and more mature age groups, freedom with the dress code, lockers, freedom to choose classes (honors vs. regular), extra curriculars, and sports. The kids care a lot more about your socioeconomic status even with uniforms implemented. While those dynamics are swirling, relationships and dating are priority number one.

Who is the cutest? Who is dating the cutest? When did they break up? How long have they been together? Have they kissed? Who's cheating on who with who? Most fights even stem from these adolescent relationships. A little out of the scope of school, church was about the same thing. Not just money but, relationships. Who was cute and who was dating who? Reflecting back on how busy I was in middle school between school, homework, tennis lessons, band, piano, band concerts, etc. I still had time to mostly focus on relationships. Insane right?

I couldn't have deep conversations with anyone except the person I was dating at the time. I would just unload onto them, needing a venting session or someone reliable to be able to converse with. I can look back now and see how irrational my demands were for 24/7 availability because I often times neeeded someone to talk to. My eyes weren't open enough to evaluate my relationships until one got physical.

I was a junior in high school I couldn't believe the episode even happened. Honestly, I don't even remember how the disagreement arose. I'm sure I have a journal entry about it. After it happened, I remember leaving the room, walking outside to breathe. I called my mom but, I just cried on the phone because no one else was answering and I couldn't call my grandma. I didn't love myself even a little bit to be in any sort of relationship. Friendships, partnerships, and situationships alike should have been far away from my mind. These various relationships exasterbated my depression and anxiety in ways I could have never imagined.

Family Dynamics

Academics were always the quickest way to get the attention of my family. I've already mentioned why. Outside of that we weren't bragged on for much. The polar opposite of that was to have their attention for negative reasons. For example, someone having a child out of wedlock, someone dropping out of high school, participating in same sex relationships, or shacking up, living with the person you were dating while not married. Relationships were always a sticky point in my family because whether you wanted it or not you would get their opinions and barrage of questions. When the questioning begins it automatically makes you defensive. Thoughts that frequented my brain space were "Do they think I can't make my own intelligent decisions?", "Do they not trust they parented me correctly?" The posture of being on the defensive automatically has you on the side of the person you are dating. You have dealt with it the entirety of your life, the person you brought in hasn't. You always want your family to like who you are dating.

That was one factor in my dating downfall. I fell into the trap of being so busy defending my date that I didn't receive a chance to see if I wanted to be with them. By the time, I figured out I wanted to leave them I was in too deep and invested. That caused me to remain in relationships that far surpassed their expiration date. My issue in the relationship came in when they mentioned marriage. I needed to see how they would be around my family if they were going to marry me. I guess by mentioning marriage you do sign up to be grilled by your significant other's family. In my experience though with friends they are no where near as intertwined with their families as I am with mine. People are used to just meeting people in your household with me it's my household and my grandmother's siblings. Since I was a kid on Sunday all of us attended church together. In addition to that, we had family dinners post service. There was never a question of when you would see your cousin again. You knew! That makes it not strange for the people I'm with to meet them. We already said my home relationships were strained so we skipped right over that. To escape that and have an authentic dating life meant leaving town.

If you've lived in a small town, you know all information gets around swiftly. Old people watching through the windows being the ultimate neighborhood watch. After being at my residential school, my family only knew what I told them and what they saw posted on my social media wall. Which at that time was a TON but, nothing they would understand. Me dating who I wanted when I wanted and being able to spend time with them nearly 24/7. I felt pretty invincible. Now the issue I was running into was the guys I wanted to date didn't want to date me. At this time, I was very forward and if I liked you, you knew it. I had it pinpointed in my head that if I didn't tell them they may never know I was interested, and we would have wasted valuable time.

We could blame romantic comedies specifically for this. The story usually started with a couple being best friends since they were kids. They had never considered dating each other until either they were about to marry their significant other or they accidentally kissed or touched in a certain way. I used that logic. I decided to completely skip over the friendship stage I saw it as wasted time. If we immediately dated, we would become friends in the process. I was rarely not in a relationship. This way of thinking caused strain on a lot of my friendship because all of my best friends were guys.

One I met in middle school and had been friends with ever since. By the time, I was at my residential school he was in the military. We still talked regularly though via instant messaging. We flirted together when we were single but never dated. He never went that extra step. Another friend of mine, a guy was in college during the time I was in school but, he was near to me. He would visit sometimes when he did, I dropped everything to go talk to him, who I was dating included. What kept me interested so long was the fact that regardless of if he had a girlfriend or not, he still came and talked to me for hours. I couldn't compute it in my brain and still can't. Why would a guy in college with a bartending job and his own apartment want to drive across town to visit hours with a 10th, 11th, and 12th grader? I only just recently ended this friendship because we would still talk for hours. After so long you learn that it's not that person isn't making the decision. That person has made the decision repeatedly and you have failed to register the decision. YOU WERE NOT CHOSEN! Even with that in front of me, I still felt chosen because he was spending time with me. The cycle of this continued many times with many people.

My last guy best friend, I met when I went to my school orientation. We were glued to the phone and each other until I was too pushy about wanting him to be mine. He had a crush on my roommate at the time. It never worked out. We still hung out hours on end just talking. At one point, he stopped being as social and only focused on his schoolwork. Adrimable for him because post graduation he entered a prestigious military school. We lost touch until this past year. "Back like we never left," my favorite RnB singer would say. That mentality though took away the time I should have been learning about myself. Not that I would have known how to do that at that time but, focusing on my studies would have been a start. Relationships overtook my academics up until my masters program. Munchkin was born then and it was grindtime. Freedom before motherhood to me meant being with the love of my life and living happily ever after somewhere outside of Alabama. Only visiting my family for certain holidays out of the year. Otherwise having my own existence with my family.

Louisiana

In college, although I was living a typical life of fun, partying, and drinking. I stayed in God's Word. I had joined a local church there and bonded with the members. It was eye opening to me to learn a new culture of family, fun, and football. In Alabama we had football: War Eagle or Crimson Tide. This was different, instead of being head to head they were united all rooting for the Saints. I had never seen more fleur de lis in my life. It's in all the home décor, grocery stores, and fast food chains. This house was united. No matter when the game was everyone watched and cheered win or lose.

My roommate at the time lived on quite a bit of land in the country. Her parents had a house and her grandparents lived next door. I spent lots of time with their family not just doing errands but talking and enjoying each other. I would say 90% of our time together was by the bonfire or fishing. It was like after Friday at three school and work did not exist. The only thing on the schedule was church Sunday morning. They were catholic but, I went with them to get the experience. It was an interesting visit. How often do you get to attend a different religion's service and then ask a million questions after without the fear of offending them. If you didn't know the largest majority religion in southern Louisiana is Catholic followed by Christians. Catholic culture is all around. It's even tied into Mardi Gras. Regardless, I was able to be 100% me and everyone was okay with it. Maybe that was the truth or perhaps only percieved. It was the first time I began to have women's bible study with my church and get to explore my faith deeper and share life with others in honesty.

My drinking and eating during this time were horrendous. Not because I liked to drink but somehow by landing in my college dorm lobby, I was linked up with multiple party crews and we all became friends. Mostly because we were all the desk clerks of the dorms and had plenty of time to kill talking and planning. Smoking was a part that. I smoked maybe for a year and a half because I thought it was cool. Everyone was getting all of this extra break time because they were a smoker. I didn't decide to stop until I moved back home. They were less into tobacco and more into cannabis. I absolutely was not. I didn't think I would ever be able to quit smoking or drinking but, I asked God to take away my smoking craving. Almost overnight it was gone. I never touched them again. A similar thing happened with drinking but that will become clear later.

Eating

Another thing that came with moving from home was access to food. Money was low and food the same. After arriving on campus, I found out not only did we have a cafeteria but, you could eat as much as you wanted. In normal public schools, you could come through the line one time. If you wanted anything extra you had to pay for it. My mom even though she didn't make much still had to pay for our school lunches so there was no go back and get more. This was new for me. Also, we always ate in large group so we would talk for ages. Get food, talk, then eat more. I also was in charge of my own snacks in my room I was able to pick out my own stuff, not having to go with what the majority wanted.

We ate so much when we were at school mostly ramen or something sweet. I was fixed on icing straight out of the container. I would be up late talking on instant messanger bored and eating. Most of my eating came from boredom not hunger. If you've ever been poor, you know you have to eat when food is available. Every event on campus usually had pizza or some other type of food. Not a healthy relationship with food when you are used to it being scarce. My size grew as my self esteem plummeted. Also, due to me quitting all sports I started yoga and weightlifting for my exercise. In that I was looking for ways to calm my inner voices. Also, I was in a dorm with four stories of girls, noisy girls. I spent most of my time in my room, the library, and on the front lawn picnic tables. Wherever the quiet was I stayed. I was seeking all of these avenues for peace when the only place I would find peace was in Christ. I was still attending church faithfully and reading God's Word but, I hadn't made it yet to a position of grattitude. I was praying about not getting into trouble, my grades, and the times I was frustrated while I was at home. Some practices continued in Lousiana onward. Peace came much later in the process of life and learning.

Chapter Five Men

The natural progression of relationships with guys went straight to sex. I have always had a ton of platonic relationships with guys. Even in my youth if that moved over to flirting my brain immediately went to dating relationships. I had been interested in sex for a while but, it didn't seem as big of a deal as people kept making it out to be. One day my time came, I was at my high school in ninth grade when I lost my virginity. The buses had just left campus and only a few people remained. My school was an hour from my home in the middle of the woods surrounded by farmland. At that age, if you didn't ride the bus, you were just left on campus, and it was assumed you had a ride, or a parent was coming at some point. This day in particular my brother and I stayed behind for basketball practice. My practice was cancelled so I had time to kill waiting on my brother. I decided to walk the grounds just to keep myself moving. I remember the band wasn't practicing that day which I thought was odd. I slowly walked past the library wishing I could go in. Finally, I decided to sit on the porch swing in the break area. No one was around. I was swinging back and forth enjoying the afternoon breeze. A guy walks up from out of the building. I watch him walk down the sidewalk past where I was to go into a different building. Suddenly, he then turned around and came back towards me.

Him: Can I sit down beside you?

Me: Sure.

Him: How is your day going?

Me: Good, bored.

Him: Why are you here?

Me: I had basketball practice, but it was cancelled. My brother has his still.

Him: Oh okay.

Silence and swinging for a while.

Him: Wanna have sex?

Me: Sure.

Walk. Walk. Walk. Done.

I didn't feel any different after, but I was scared to death that I could have gotten pregnant. Even though, I was more worried that my mom would find out. I'm not sure how but, my brother knew the next day. More blackmail fuel. I was literally telling everyone because, I was proud of it. I told my best friend the next morning on the bus. She asked me who was it. I said his name was Sam (not his actual name.) She asked me about two last names. I told her I didn't know which one but, I picked one of the two last names and went with that. I found out maybe two days later when we exchanged number that I had chosen the wrong last name. All the information I had been blabbering about was incorrect. Now, I was thinking, did that make it seem like I slept with both or sad because I didn't know his last name. Nevertheless, we got to know each other past that day. At this school, it was generational with everyone knowing everyone. It was rarely someone moving to our school unless they were kicked out from another school and forced to change. It would be weird for me to not know someone's first and last name. I moved away briefly at the beginning of my sixth grade year that I mentioned previously. I returned my 8th grade year during Christmas break before this happened in the fall.

This guy wasn't even a guy on my "I'm into you" list. There were two guys I was interested in on my bus. One that had been my crush since kindergarten. He stayed pretty close to my grandma's house, maybe a mile or two. That allowed me to see him in the summer sometimes. To see him, made for some excitement in the middle of a ton of boring days. We would smile at each other on the bus and sometimes sit together. He would butter me up and try to cop a feel. Thinking back now, that was during the time I was all about cleavage. I wore tight uncomfortable tops to make my cleavage stand out more. This was the era where we usually wore two shirts to school. A collared shirt with a tank underneath. I remember many arguments between my grandmother and I about how I wore my clothes. I didn't consider myself to be a fashionista at this time or ever. Unknowingly to me we were poor! We had five pairs of clothes, a shirt and bottom, that we rotated through the school year. All year. There was very little to be in disagreement about. Not sure when it happened but at some point, I switched to wearing just t-shirts and jeans everyday, showing nothing at all. Something to do with how uncomfortable my stepdad made me feel.

The other guy I was interested in we will call him Matt. He was too busy trying to look tough and cool to want me. He was new when I returned back to school here. He fought a lot on the bus. Typical bad boy but, we talked a TON. When I say a ton, I mean an hour and a half to and from school everyday. He is the only person still to this day with the exclusion of one person that I can have any conversation with and talk endlessly. We dated maybe one day. Exactly one day because I felt like even though we had agreed to do it he would deny me if anyone asked him. I decided to break up with him first soon as we got back on the bus that afternoon. He still holds it over my head that I broke up with him. This went on for years. Each time we were together I broke up with him. Then there were guys I was interested in, and they weren't interested in me and vice versa

Ehhhh I always had a boyfriend. One in particular was very hands on and loved public displays of affection. I loved that about him because it meant he wasn't ashamed of me. It's hard for me to look back on my story and use the word ashamed. There is no reason in the world a ninth grader should have a reason to be ashamed of herself. NONE! That's a very sad reality to face. I WAS ASHAMED! I'm pretty sure I felt that way even before I was sexually active. What was there to be ashamed of? That I liked someone? That someone wouldn't like me? That people would know either of the two.

All games. All pointless. We were dating mostly out of boredom of country living, an unchallenging curriculum, and a lack of a thought-provoking environment. This continued through high school and gratefully mostly stopped at college. The bus guy Matt remained in my life up until 2022. I never slept with him until 2012, I was 19, in college, and he had been in the military. One night and then nothing. Years of anticipation which led to a laughter filled night, some fun, and an unexpected sleepover. But no call after. I would find out a year later that we were both waiting for the other to call. Very much a lost opportunity that can't be grasped again. A major part I left out of Matt's story is during school years, although I was his confident. He would bully me. If you asked him today, he would deny it but those experience are very vivid in my memory. It was a major reason why I could never trust him fully He pinched me, hit me, and one time slapped me. He sometimes bullied my brother which still causes issues to this day. That was the hardest attachment to let go of. Mainly because it was filled with so many years of truth (at least what I thought was truth) and vulnerability. I thought that was what love was, someone who kept returning to offer their love no matter what. This guy ended up back in my life constantly around 2016.

During this last period of not talking, he had gotten married and had two boys. His wife cheated on him which resulted in divorce. During the divorce, she was pregnant. This son turned out to be his also. We decided that even though we were both interested in each other we would just have sex because he was still freshly divorced. I couldn't comprehend how he would want to get married again so soon. We settled for that arrangement to where it was so freeing to be with someone with MOST of my guards down. Even though we agreed to be casual we acted as though we were in a relationship fully. Our hold up—other than the recent divorce was my convictions about the church. I wanted to attend weekly and serve with my husband. I went through thoughts of maybe I'm the wife that's supposed to pray my husband to heaven and he will later give his life to Christ from seeing my life.

> "Likewise, wives, be subject to your own husbands, so that even if some do not obey the word, they may be won without a word by the conduct of their wives," 1 Peter 3:1 ESV[22]

Every way you could spin it, I tried to make it work logically. One thing he could not get over was that if we were going to be in a serious committed relationship the sex had to stop. I knew by that point that sex majorly affected my judgement in relationships. If the sex stayed amazing, I would

---

[22] https://bible.com/bible/59/1pe.3.1.ESV

pretty much justify any way possible to make the relationship work. So far as to compromising any other thing I valued in the relationship. He couldn't understand it, but it was the only way I could take the commitment serious on his side. I just tried to keep explaining it to him. He couldn't understand and I get that for two reasons:

1. I had before with him in relationship and sex been on and off due to my conscious and the fact that he couldn't ever be consistent. On and off. He would talk to me one week then ghost me the next week. Me days on end checking my phone waiting for his texts and calls. I was waiting for a sinful and uninterested man to fulfill his promise. The thing is I like many others who haven't yet learned their worth clung to the few I love you's over the thousands of unreturned calls, ignored social media messages, failed plans, excuses, gas and time wasted waiting. We forget how precious time is. All of that time wasted. The longer we hang on to that fairy tale the longer it darkens or blocks our view.

2. He wasn't an obedient believer but, he believed in God. Now when I'm saying believer here, I mean a few things. We all have points in our life where we thought we

were doing things correctly for God and we weren't. That's apart of the sanctification process. I will tell you all of my life I have been a believer and sometimes an obedient believer. It's like knowing a fact vs. living a life of knowing all truth about everything. Now until you have landed there you are still what folks call "straddling the fence." One foot in and one foot out. Now God tells us he reveals things to us a little at a time, so we aren't overwhelmed. He does that by acting through our experiences. I would say the largest difference between a beliver, and an obedient believer is the amount of peace.

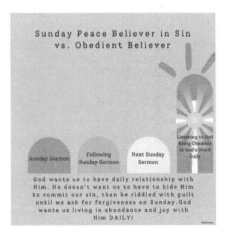

This was probably the hardest lesson for me to learn. It involved a lot of struggles within myself to say hey God says this, and you feel this. Over and over again I would plead to God, not for self discipline but for permission. The permission to be free in my sin nature. I knew that I had desires, hopes, and dreams I wanted to be satisfied in my personal life. I was asking God when I would be allowed to indulge. I wanted to find someone I could be totally free with. Share all of my wants and needs with. That person needs to be okay with it and just satisfied with pleasing me. In my normal nature, I'm a spoiling sort of partner. I love to buy gifts and surprise the other person but, I don't think I've asked one person how they would like to be loved. I have to admit something right now that is hard:

THE ABUSER WAS RIGHT! I AM SELFISH! The one thing I never wanted to be. Some people say soulmates are not the ones you end up married to but, the ones who reveals the most about you to yourself. I wanted permission to pick the person I should be with and let myself believe that love would be enough. But it's not enough. Let me be clear: LOVE IS NOT ENOUGH FOR A RELATIONSHIP WITH ANY HUMAN! The only relationship where love is enough is with God: Father, Son, and Holy Spirit. There is so much more that causes a relationship to be a success. This taught me through about 17 years that love was not enough. Hallelujah I'm free. I now after years of therapy realized what I really sought after was what Christ has to offer. The total package:

Love:

> "The Lord will fulfill his purpose for me; your steadfast love, O Lord, endures forever. Do not forsake the work of your hands." Psalm 138:8 ESV[23]

God's love is never ending. It doesn't fluctuate as his moods change. There is no variable that changes it. God's love is the same and constant for you forever.

> ""For God so loved the world, that he gave his only Son, that whoever believes in him should not perish but have eternal life." John 3:16 ESV[24]

God sacrifices for us to prove His love. God used His own Son to reopen the lines of communication between us and Him.

---

[23] https://bible.com/bible/59/psa.138.8.ESV
[24] https://bible.com/bible/59/jhn.3.16.ESV

> "But God shows his love for us in that while
> we were still sinners, Christ died for us."
> Romans 5:8 ESV[25]

God shows the ultimate forgiveness for all mankind
by instead of destroying us like we deserve. He
pondered a solution to help our life here on earth
through Christ and the Holy Spirit.

Our God loves us and cares about our lives. If
our life here on earth was meaningless then God
would have never sent down His son to die for us. He
could have just destroyed us and started over. He
said, "no" this time I will flip the script. Since they
can't keep from sinning on their own, I will send
them help and a perfect sacrifice to fulfill that
requirement.

Honor:

> "Honor everyone. Love the brotherhood. Fear
God. Honor the emperor." 1 Peter 2:17   ESV[26]

> "Strength and dignity are her clothing, and
she laughs at the time to come." Proverbs   31:25
ESV[27]

---

[25] https://bible.com/bible/59/rom.5.8.ESV
[26] https://bible.com/bible/59/1pe.2.17.ESV
[27] https://bible.com/bible/59/pro.31.25.ESV

"Humble yourselves, therefore, under the mighty hand of God so that at the proper time he may exalt you,"1 Peter 5:6 ESV[28]

"Yet you have made him a little lower than the heavenly beings and crowned him with glory and honor." Psalm 8:5 ESV[29]

God wants to lift us up to a higher platform than just a sinner. If we continue to choose to sit in our sin and not repent, then we are living a life of destruction over honor. God has called us to be more. He called us to be His family then to treat others as if they are in His family as well. When we treat people that way, we show them something different from what they are receiving from the world. The more difficult and evil our world becomes the more vital and easy our jobs become. We are showing the love of God, showing honor to the body, and lives He gave us by being obedient to what He says.

Worth:

"A gracious woman gets honor, and violent men get riches." Proverbs 11:16 ESV[30]

---

[28] https://bible.com/bible/59/1pe.5.6.ESV
[29] https://bible.com/bible/59/psa.8.5.ESV
[30] https://bible.com/bible/59/pro.11.16.ESV

"For no one ever hated his own flesh, but nourishes and cherishes it, just as Christ does the church," Ephesians 5:29 ESV[31]

"You will increase my greatness and comfort me again." Psalm 71:21 ESV[32]

"For the Lord God is a sun and shield; the Lord bestows favor and honor. No good thing does he withhold from those who walk uprightly." Psalm 84:11 ESV[33]

Following honor, it's similar but think of how worthy it is to God that He can have the light of His love shine throughout His creation. I see sharing God's Word and love as the world starts off pitch black. God staring at it then seeing one little light pop up and He smiles. Then like an ant that little light starts moving around sharing its light with others on its various paths. Dim lights begin to sparkle while following their own paths. The lights grow brighter and multiply throughout the earth. This causes God so much joy and gives worth to our journey.

Purpose:

---

[31] https://bible.com/bible/59/eph.5.29.ESV
[32] https://bible.com/bible/59/psa.71.21.ESV
[33] https://bible.com/bible/59/psa.84.11.ESV

"And we know that for those who love God all things work together for good, for those who are called according to his purpose." Romans 8:28 ESV[34]

"Who saved us and called us to a holy calling, not because of our works but because of his own purpose and grace, which he gave us in Christ Jesus before the ages began," 2 Timothy 1:9 ESV[35]

"Go therefore and make disciples of all nations, baptizing them in the name of the Father and of the Son and of the Holy Spirit," Matthew 28:19 ESV[36]

"For I know the plans I have for you, declares the Lord, plans for welfare and not for evil, to give you a future and a hope." Jeremiah 29:11 ESV[37]

Not only do we bring God joy for His purpose and glory. He has things working in our favor and for our good. He has tapped us on the shoulder at formation to say this one is my daughter or son. The light clicks when it's time to plug in and get to work.

---

[34] https://bible.com/bible/59/rom.8.28.ESV
[35] https://bible.com/bible/59/2ti.1.9.ESV
[36] https://bible.com/bible/59/mat.28.19.ESV
[37] https://bible.com/bible/59/jer.29.11.ESV

Our works though are not without reward. There is a journey sometimes to get the reward, but my favorite reward of all time so far is beyond human comprehension peace.

Those experiences weren't bad now. In the end, they pointed me to my real relationship with Christ that He was longing to have with me. It hurt but, to be free now was worth it. Moment to moment living with Him but that's not all. I have been in every type of unhealthy relationship you can imagine. Abuse. Physical. Mental. Verbal. Manipulation. Scamming. Trapping. A beard[38]. Blow up doll. Housing. Transportation. It all led to this moment!

I am now empathetic when I listen about the relationships of others. Before, I heard he said, she said. My thought process was okay, what side am I on and how can we prove that to the opposing side. Now I see her hurts, his hurts and how although they both want the same things they can't reach each other because of unhealthy coping skills and miscommunication. Although, I see it that way that doesn't make it easier or cause me to make the relationship better. What it does do, is let me point who I'm talking to towards Christ. Explaining what He

---

[38] Slang for a disguise

offers knowing it has nothing to do with their boyfriend or girlfriend relationship. As the one I talk to becomes healthier they can decide for themselves if this is a relationship they should stay involved in or not. Speaking into the lives of others is so much easier when you aren't forcing them to do something. For example, leave their boyfriend.

It won't be easy to progress the relationship forward if the other partner chooses to heal. Even if they do, they may find with the healing, the relationship is not needed. That's not the end of the world but, the beginning of their story. This being the path God has for their ultimate purpose. I as a believer, support a person through that growth, healing, and hurt. You pray that God will see them to the other side of their valley of the shadow of death, woes, or trauma. I and you can help others escape their patterns of behavior and get onto the path God has for their lives! I can tell you a few ways I have put that into practice. I have a few people I would call friends and about a million people I would call acquaintances. Even the people I would call friends get the.........chapter 7.

Chapter Six Achievement

We discussed I tried running away, distracting myself with men, the last and final thing I tried was to achieve my way out of this hole. I knew since kindergarten that education would be important in my life. My mom and cousins were all in college when I was growing up. An aunt of mine was going to school to be a nurse practitioner. I always knew I was going to college. I kept straight A's for quite a while. Within and outside of my family I was known for my grades. Not to mention at my first school I was lacking the stimulating environment. I didn't have to try hard to succeed.

One example of this outside of report cards, honors days, and church recognition was my mother's job. I would attend higher level courses with her students in high school and keep up. My favorite class was by a friend of mine's dad. I've always wanted to be a pediatrician but this science class solitified that. Quite a bit of the class had to do with the memorization of scientific instruments but, it was interesting to me. Like previously mentioned before, in middle school things started to be divided. This was the time you chose what track you would finish out on. There were three types: college, normal, or trade. That was the same year I changed schools. English became read this book and provide a book report. Math was more thought provoking. That would be the first time I've read through one of my favorite books "The Secret Garden[39]." I became friends with my social studies teacher where we learned every country of continent of Africa along with weekly projects i.e. making chocolate covered crickets, baking pastry to make heiroglyphics[40].

It was also during this time my world began to open up. I had a chance to spend two weeks overseas with other selected students from my school. Only one other attended and then my social studies teacher. We spent 14 days exploring London, Ireland, and Wales. I've wanted to go back and live there ever since. The idea of living abroad pushed me forward to what I thought would be the dream. Being a writer. I still have a dream of getting my doctorate at a college there. We managed to fit in a few

---

[39] Burnett, Frances Hodgson, 1849-1924. The Secret Garden. Boston, MA: D. R. Godine, 1987.
[40] "Written in, constituting, or belonging to a system of writing mainly in pictorial characters" https://www.merriam-webster.com/dictionary/hieroglyphics

colleges and kiss the Blarney Stone[41]. During that time, I learned it might have been rare to see a black person there but, it was still possible.

My awards for clarinet and writing started near this. My first poem ever written was awarded. I recited it maybe at three events and won all three. From then on, it was confirmed I should be a writer. Doctor first but definitely a writer at some point. Most of my friends weren't into school as much but that didn't bother me. Imagine being the oddball out smarty, getting ripped from your school as soon as you were about to graduate eighth grade you get tossed back into an unstimulating environment. I was disappointed to learn our highest class would be Chemistry 1.

Being placed back in the fishbowl made me stand out even more. I was moved up one grade in math and stayed a year ahead. Honors for everything I could be in and playing basketball. I was still bored out of my mind. This is when books became the

---

[41] "Legends about the Stone's origin emerged, each as plausible as the next. It was said to have been the stone used by Jacob as a pillow when he dreamed of the ladder extending up to heaven with angels ascending and descending on it, and that it was brought from the Holy Land after the Crusades." Blarney Castle Blarney, Cork, Ireland https://blarneycastle.ie/blarney-stone/#:~:text=Blarney%20Stone%20History&text=Legends%20about%20the%20Stone's%20origin,Holy%20Land%20after%20the%20Crusades.

escape. I was wrapped up in the wizarding world and schoolgirl romance books. People began to treat me as an adult because I was intelligent, not allowing me a childhood. I would learn whatever they were learning. I took notes wherever I went. I checked out MCAT books in the summer to bide my time and not get rusty.

This invitation to a new school sounded good but, I wasn't interested in starting over with a new friend group. Until one day I was so upset with my home life I just said, "let's do it." I was going into tenth grade being able to take pretty much any class I wanted outside of graduation requirements. We worked on trimesters so for a light load you could do five classes per trimester. That's 15 classes a year. I decided to keep trekking forward into pre-med with a concentration in biology. I debated between a second minor of Spanish and chemistry. Chemistry was the easier choice if not for the labs. Biology labs made for messy work and long hours after normal class schedule hours. We dredged water from the bay in kayaks, went to secluded areas of forestation to find various species of plants, found invertebrates below the beach sand, and went out after dark to study nocturnal animals. This was all in high school. Not to mention a year of physics and organic chemistry to graduate. I enjoyed it all it was just a lot to compute mentally with hormones and my social life in the mix. I ended up doing a distinction in biology and history. I have always been facinated with history. I took many classes just out of curiosity ending up with a distinction of six extra classes beyond that subject requirement.

In college, I stayed on that track for a while. I entered with my major being pre-med biology with a minor in Spanish. I was enjoying Spanish but, it frustrated me. While the vocabulary and memorization came to me easily the conjugations and sentence formation did not. I gave up that dream to focus exclusively on core classes. I thought the labs were a lot before, but this was more. Now I was getting on large fishing tub boats scraping the ocean floor to find invertebrates to come back and look at under the microscope.

My favorite class was probably somewhere between English and microbiology. Microbiology had a ton of labs and information to learn but, much calm surrounded those technical aspects that I loved. I would simply often be burned out even while being encouraged by my instructors. During my junior year, my job cut my hours for the summer. I couldn't afford my apartment. I had to come back home to Alabama to finish school. That devastated me. This was the one place I did not want to be. Back under so much influence and suppression of self. After one year of hating biology and pre-med there and losing a ton of credits. I was swooned away by political science and philosophy.

The teachers knew and cared for their students. My future looked bright there. I finally changed majors and never turned back. I didn't want to do American Politics with all of the law students. I was fatigued with that avenue. Being world travelled I knew some day I would want to work at the United Nations[42]. If not there then as a diplomat. I began to work towards taking the foreign service officer test to go down the diplomat path. I learned there would be a verbal portion. By this time, I had taken speech. While I loved the class I hated public speaking. I was in my head thinking I had already taken too long to complete my bachelors. I had to decide what my master's degree would be in.

My instuctors wanted me to do public administration or vere into Russian or Middle Eastern politics. Those were my areas of interest. I even had my amazing economics teacher ask me to go into their master's program. Decisions, decisions. When it

---

[42] "One place where the world's nations can gather together, discuss common problems and find shared solutions." https://www.un.org/en/about-us

came down to what I considered I would need for he future, I knew I hated public speaking. I chose strategic communications thinking it would be a more amplified version of speech and papers. What it actually was dealt with social media management, crisis management, and blog management. Still working on a voice but, not the voice I was intending to strengthen. I graduated every time with no excitement or impact. I knew it was just time to plan for the next thing I needed to accomplish. The only thing I knew at that point was I had a baby to provide for and I needed to get climbing that corporate ladder to get to a place we would be able to afford her needs.

For three years, I applied to jobs daily. Nothing. I completed at least 20 applications each day. I received maybe five interviews in that time. I thought, "here I am again stuck." I looked for a church that wasn't my family's after the millionth time God had told me to leave. One I had in mine was one I used to go to when I started my pharmacy job on days, I couldn't make the 45 minute drive to church. They had an eight am service. I went and never left. The service time had change but, it didn't phase me. I jumped in headfirst.

To make a long story shorter, my first job came from a contact at that church. Something I never thought I would be doing. Due to things that took place with my uncle previously mentioned before I knew at some point I would work with veterans. This job gave me a chance to work with active duty military. Two years in, I was still trying to prove myself above and beyond the compliments and praises I was receiving daily from my coworkers. I asked God for a job that would allow me to have the mental, physical, and financial capabilities to be there for my daughter. It took two years for me to realize I was living the dream I prayed for. No longer needing to strive but, remaining dependable and consistent. I had already moved into a management position and was successful at it. I had the brain space now to write. I can't tell you how long I begged to have room in my brain to write my books. I have that. It wasn't about my accomplishments though it was about the position God was in my life and how well I was listening to His instruction and adjusting.

Through this journey, I saw that it would be an endless list of the things I wanted to accomplish to make it where I thought I wanted to be. There were rare times I had a true friend. Even though I was intelligent and knowingly able. I had no joy. My only joy was being away from home because I could be myself. Much of my time until then, I was in the pit of death. I only felt full and, in my purpose when studying God's Word. I felt being in His Word would be a great job for me at the same time not knowing what it meant or what it would look like. I've spent years trying to figure it out. Reading God's Word was a safe place to be. I always held on to the Bible clinging to it in desperation sometimes. I felt closest to God while reading it. I felt I He was open to my questions, knowing the questions may or may not be answered in this lifetime. This was my joy. I had a taste but, didn't know if I was truly there yet.

Part Three: Resolve & Rest

Chapter Seven L. C. L.

Listen. . .

Contemplate. . .

Listen. . .

L. C. L. is the method I use to be an active spiritual listener to others. I listen to what is concerning them. I contemplate but don't comment. Then, I listen some more. I notice that we sometimes talk so much that we miss the opportunity for someone to learn something on their own. We so badly want to be right or solve their problem, including myself. I would say more than anything people just want to be heard. Not studied, not diagnosed, not problem solved, just listened to. I use this skill mostly in two ways:

1. When I volunteer:

When we choose to volunteer, for the most part it is because we want to do something for someone else outside of ourselves. One place I volunteer is on an ultrasound bus that provides free ultrasounds for the under and uninsured. They get a chance to see and connect with their baby in the first trimester. Most doctors won't see them until they are at 12 weeks of pregnancy. At that point, they have only had an at home pregnancy test to confirm pregnancy and nothing else. These girls and women come in from many differing situations. Some married, some unplanned pregnancies, some overwhelmed, some surprised by twins when they are already raising children alone. My solution when I don't know what to do or say, is to listen and listen more. It helps. They know at least one person is supporting them and from me they can get to Christ. ISN'T THAT GREAT NEWS "THROUGH ME THEY CAN GET TO CHRIST!" That hit my heart hard. Thank you, Holy Spirit! HALLELUJAH!

I've always felt there was something I could be doing to help young girls. I never knew what it was supposed to be. This opportunity fell right into my lap. In not knowing, I didn't push away from the calling. Let me say I didn't run away cautiously because I run away quite often from my writing. I thought let's try this opportunity and see how it goes. I could always switch to something different if it didn't pan out. My first idea of where I wanted to volunteer was well received and planned. I could never line it up with my schedule to make it happen. This though was perfect: I could hear and interact with the stories and testimonies of these women. I was also encouraged by the women I worked side by side with. Hand in hand with the help of Christ and the Holy Spirit that always fills the bus. Blessings, joy, and light all around. All of this does not mean it was easy. These girls came in with their hard stories. They had been carrying these stories in their body coming to us needing help. The type of help though was yet to be determined until they opened up to us. This though was not the only time I was able to use listen, contemplate, listen.

2. With my daughter:

My child deserves a whole book about her already at the age of seven. She is one of my greatest blessings. I knew what type of mother I wanted to be since the age of eight. My daughter wasn't planned at the time she was conceived but prior to that she was prayed for by name about six months earlier. I became a mother at 23. I found out I was pregnant at two weeks. This was early to find out and I was in complete shock. Fast forward this sassy, strong, independent munchkin of mine is amazing. She's an artist, gymnast, author, scholar, engineer, chef, cosmetologist, songwriter, among many other things.

The most important thing for me as her mother was to be in a place that I could be there for her mentally, physically, and emotionally. Success has arrived. I can't tell you from the time she's been born how many heartfelt conversations, belly laughs, and overcoming of struggles that me and this girl have been through. I am all the better because of it. Her too. I recently was at bible study, and she asked me did I talk about her at all.

Me: You know I did girl.

Arpi: What did you say?

Me: I said I had really been enjoying watching anime with you and belly laughing at the same things because we don't normally find the same things funny. Also, singing and dancing together.

Arpi: Okay, did you cry?

Me: Yes, hold up! How do you know that?

Arpi: Mama, you always cry when you talk about something joyful.

THE FACT THAT AT SEVEN YEARS OLD MY DAUGHTER KNOWS WHAT JOYFUL IS AND SEES IT WHEN SHE THINKS OF HER MAMA! That means everything to me. She has seen me sad, but, that she views me as joyful is Christ filled. I can probably count on one hand how many times I could say that my mom and grandmother together have been happy much less joyful.

My Introduction to Therapy

Seems like a great place to tell you why I started therapy in the first place. Some background information, my mother has worked in the mental health field all of my life. I always knew what therapy was. Her first job I remembered was A.I.M (Abstinence in Motion). Where she would go to different schools and do presentations about sex before marriage, STDs, etc. It was boring for us as young as we were but, it did get us out of the house often on weekends. After that, she worked about an hour from where we lived in a group home for the mentally challenged. I think she loved the job it was just too far away from home. The job she stayed at the longest, she counseled high schoolers. We stayed on the premises 8am-5pm, 5pm-8pm, and weekends in the summer. It was fun and tiring for all of us. The thing that bothered me the most was she always had time for those kids and her fellow employees but not us.

There were many things I wanted to talk to her about. She wasn't available to talk to. I'm sure most people can relate to trying to talk to someone and they keep stopping you in the middle of your story to say, "one second". "Can we talk later?" Etc. IT HURTS! You are never important and that's where I lived. In a place of no importance. I would see kids go in her office for sessions 30 minutes to an hour. I would be left in the hallway waiting. Same thing happened when she had a man. We would remain in the waiting room. This caused me to begin to resent my mother and how she spent her time. She was in a sorority. We spent endless hours in the car or in another room waiting. Sorority work and meetings took up other weekends. I felt alone. I already explained my brother and I had a strained relationship. At the same time, my mother was too busy for me.

This was the reason I started therapy in the ninth grade. I plainly put did not want to hate my mom. Intuitive for my age to know that I needed to seek help for that. I'm not sure if I was aware enough to know if I needed help or if I just knew I had a ton of built-up anger that needed to come out. I knew I could talk to a counselor because, I had seen it before. Counseling about my mother became pretty irrelevant because I was now at my residential school without my family. I only went home for school breaks and summers. During those breaks, I knew when the end date of the torture would be. I didn't even unpack my bags when I came home. I would be a recluse, read, and text all day and night. What did I have to look forward to there?

The topic changed with the counselor to being about school stressors, friends, and relationships. My sophomore year, I entered a toxic relationship, not sure how long into that relationship we started couples counseling, but we did. The importance of counseling stuck with me. In college, when I moved to Louisiana, I found the counseling center immediately. I ended up with an intern counselor this time. I didn't mind. We bonded well. This was also my first time Having a black counselor. A different dynamic but it made me relax a little. I came in with the same goal of not wanting to hate my mom. What really drove this goal for me was the fact I knew in the Bible it was forbidden.

Old Testament

> ""Honor your father and your mother, that your days may be long in the land that the Lord your God is giving you."" Exodus 20:12 ESV[43]

> ""'Honor your father and your mother, as the Lord your God commanded you, that your days may be long, and that it may go well

---

[43] https://bible.com/bible/59/exo.20.12.ESV

with you in the land that the Lord your God is giving you."" Deuteronomy 5:16 ESV[44]

"Every one of you shall revere his mother and his father, and you shall keep my Sabbaths: I am the Lord your God." Leviticus 19:3 ESV[45]

New Testament

"For God commanded, 'Honor your father and your mother,' and, 'Whoever reviles father or mother must surely die.'" Matthew 15:4 ESV[46]

""Honor your father and mother, and, you shall love your neighbor as yourself."" Matthew 19:19 ESV[47]

"Children, obey your parents in the Lord, for this is right. "Honor your father and mother", "that it may go well with you and that you may live long in the land." Fathers, do not provoke your children to anger, but bring them up in the discipline and instruction of the Lord." Ephesians 6:1-4 ESV[48]

---

[44] https://bible.com/bible/59/deu.5.16.ESV
[45] https://bible.com/bible/59/lev.19.3.ESV
[46] https://bible.com/bible/59/mat.15.4.ESV
[47] https://bible.com/bible/59/mat.19.19.ESV
[48] https://bible.com/bible/59/eph.6.1-4.ESV

"You know the commandments: 'Do not commit adultery, Do not murder, Do not steal, Do not bear false witness, Honor your father and mother.'"" Luke 18:20 ESV[49]

As a small kid I knew that no matter what mistakes I made I would make it to heaven. Not because I knew I wouldn't make mistakes but that I would be blessed to repair them before it was my time to go. I not for one second knowing this took any second for granted or felt I could do anything I wanted as a result of that. Thank God He always weighed down my conscience and use my emotions to keep me near to Him.

To fix this I needed someone to listen to me. Really listen to me and give me an objective opinion. Counseling was my pathway to that. One thing I think was important to note that contributed to my anger was:

1. Everyone knew my mom.
    Me knowing everyone already knew my mom, they already had their own personal feelings or views about her which would prevent me from speaking freely. I made friends and acquaintances with friends of hers, coworkers, employees, students, even mere

[49] https://bible.com/bible/59/luk.18.20.ESV

acquaintances. Some of the responses I received was "you know she does a lot," "you know your mother loves you," or "you know she has a lot on her plate." Coworkers would say I could talk to them but would turn around and repeat what I said back to her. One employee of hers had similar views as me about my mom but, we only spoke of minor annoyances.

I dated some of her students but, they only saw this beautiful woman who my mother was. Also, that she was the better more interesting, sexier prize. It led to conflict a lot in my relationships that they would talk about my mom being "fine, beautiful" and the things they would say about her body. "Why am I even trying," was my thought. She was the unattainable goal making me the closest they could get to her.

2. Family.

At one point, I thought because of the history between my grandmother and my mother she would prove to be the easiest to talk to. This ended up not being the case. She would listen but, this would be the first and repeated time that she would interrupt me. I would be shocked every time. I just knew this time I would be in the right. Nope, I was wrong simply because I wasn't honoring my mother by venting. My grandma always encouraged me to forgive and move on. I just wanted to be heard. God knew what was happening to me and I felt He would not be pleased either.

I explained that I felt unseen, unheard, and irrelevant to my family. I still do. I would detail to my counselor that every time I tried to voice my concerns to my mother, I would get so frustrated. That would cause me to cry because, I couldn't argue with her and say the things I wanted. I had to stay censored and honoring. That crying made me felt weak because I was holding it in. I was hurt again because I wasn't being heard. Again, my feelings weren't important. Again, I would be silenced.

At some point in middle school, I realized I expressed myself a lot better in writing than speaking. I began to write multipage letters of how I felt. I would speak carefully trying not to trigger her or disrespect her. Imagine trying to do that in eighth grade. When I finished, I would slide it under her door. She would read it and eventually call me in to discuss it.

From that letter, she would pick certain parts to bring up and I would have to explain what I meant. It would be quickly rebuttled with a tear filled "I do everything I can for you." That statement would make me feel guilty about writing the letter in the first place. I would then cry. Apologize for saying anything. Then, all would go back to normal. Me being ignored, not mattering. This cycle continued through my adulthood maybe through college when I found this counselor. By that point, I decided to give up on that relationship and continue to move forward with the person who would listen, my grandmother.

I would call my grandmother multiple times a day to tell her about my grades or when I was upset about something. She would write me through the mail all of my life. That's how I view love. Someone using every avenue to proclaim their love showing how they care. I've gone to lengths to tell you how I feel about her already, I won't repeat it. The relationship with my grandmother being so right, does that mean what my mom did was wrong? Hmmmm hard to say.

You often hear people say, "we have to take it on a case-by-case basis." Let's present it this way:

In 2023, I see my mom as a:

- A survivor of abuse
- Late educated – college in her 30s
- A woman who lost her dreams of modeling when she had kids

- A depressed young mom
- An overwhelmed young mom
- A single mom of two
- A single mom trying to learn & protect her son
- A multiple time divorcee

A lot of my emotions are intertwined within these.

I see myself as:

- A survivor of abuse
- An overcomer of obstacles
- A hard worker
- A divorcee of a scammer
- A truth seeker
- A disability advocate
- An advocate for silenced women
- A depression, anxiety, and PTSD fighter
- A hopeless romantic
- A FREAKING AMAZING MOM

Some of those positive things about myself were formed out of the bad I was presented. I've had times of no guidance, times of being left alone when I should have been supervised, and times of being in places seen as safe but, wasn't. Can I say it was wrong to have a child be alone, lonely, and unheard? Yes! Can I say it made me who I am? Yes! Therapy turned my hurts, abuse, and loneliness into the power of knowing myself. That information allowed me to know how I fit into the body of Christ. I can know why Christ came and died for me. I can stand on top of that pile of crap and say, "BUT GOD!" BUT MY GOD ALMIGHTY DELIVERED!

Motivation: Daughter

This left therapy as my avenue for a sounding board. I didn't want my child to be affected by my shortcomings of living in pain. I knew I was not perfect and never would be. I knew my patience was short. I was open to fixing other things I would discover in therapy to come. Those undiscovered things took time. The biggest was paying attention to my emotions and how my body felt at different times. This came out mostly in my dating life, with my family (inner and extended), and in my parenting.

I knew kids could feel your emotions, even babies. I started early with the calming techniques. I had the most amazing pregnancy. I ate extremely healthy. Lots of fruits and vegetables. My doctor allowed me to use milkshakes to get my milk servings in. I had plenty of peach milkshakes from this local fast-food spot with grilled nuggets. I haven't had the nuggets since. I couldn't cook meat because it turned my stomach. Daily I would do yoga, play classical music, took many naps, and even read to the baby in utero. I had a scent picked out for her nursery it was grapefruit. I would burn that candle and go into that room daily to read Bible stories to baby. Sometimes I would get a nap on the floor in there. I wanted that room to be surrounded by love, God, and positivity when she arrived.

Fast forward to toddlerhood she loved when I watched sermons on TV. She would pretend to be a preacher. Also, 150% full of energy. We went outside daily to draw with chalk, paint, explore, or pick flowers. We watched all of her developmental shows together and did mama and me yoga with music time. We read tons of books. Her birthday is after Labor Day so in the south you have to wait one additional year to start school. We had the pleasure of doing Pre-K twice. Kindergarten started all of the mommy issues. The movement from being the boss of my child's life to only an advocate for her. It was a large jump for me. Gratefully by that point we had an amazing relationship where she would tell me any and everything. Her teachers and I had great relationships as well where I could get clarification or additional information. This year she is in first grade. I can begin to see that the traits I noticed with her before are going to stick. In preschool, her favorite thing was to bring any left over snacks from this private school to the homeless people on our interstate exit. This year she told me how happy it made her that she used to do that.

She still likes to feed the homeless. It bled over into her wanting to feed all her friends on her school bus, including the bus driver. All of the 300 students at her school are her friends and love her. She draws them pictures, makes them cards, and brings them gifts. A heart of gold. Equally important with that heart she knows when and how to stand up for herself. I have never been able to do that but, I am ecstatic that she can and will. She knows she has to have mutual respect in her friendships. She even gives them grace which is more beautiful. There was recently an incident on the bus. I had to bring it to the attention of the principal. While mentioning the names of the people involved, she repeated one name and said, "I'm going to give her one more chance. Don't mention her name." I did ask her was she sure but, I was proud she had that discernment. Those little moments are important as a parent as a check of your child's values. Even this morning we discussed, I know you think of things but, they all shouldn't leave your mouth. She said, "mama, can I just be honest." I said, "of course, always but, I still need you to think about if it's respectful or will it hurt that person's feelings first." She didn't like it but, she understood.

I speak with my daughter like an adult. I always have. She is highly intelligent. I treat her as such. It has improved our communication greatly because she isn't afraid of telling me her emotions. This allows me to help her to regulate them better. She used to cry and not talk. After years of saying, "I can't help you if you can't communicate to me the problem," it finally works. Parents don't give up. It may seem like your child doesn't need guidance because they are mature for their age. That doesn't mean they aren't hungry for direction. Even at our current age we need advice on things. If you don't give your children guidance, they will get it from somewhere whether that is from other kids at school, observing you, observing other adults, TV or music. The environment they are in also matters. I took my daughter two weeks ago to a tea house and she asked me, "Mom, can I be excused from the table?" I immediately did a double take because where did she learn that from? It came from something she had watched. It stuck. If we put our kids in places that require more. They will show up.

Counseling is still apart of my life as a stronger woman. A stronger woman I am because I saw a young mother struggle. Due to me enduring this loneliness, I was able to hone in on something I love: reading, writing, and learning. God turns our struggles into ministry. My loneliness has been turned into poetry of feeling for all. My writing has been turned into ministry. This being my first fully fleshed out book about Christ I can confidently say this will be my ministry because, HE MADE IT POSSIBLE! He gave me the words and life to tell you. There is more to come. Just say yes to listen to God speaking to you. To heal you. To letting him work.

Chapter Eight Hope, Faith, & Trust

How much time do we waste complaining while people suffer? I have been in situations where I have cried at public occurences where I wanted to help and couldn't. Some of them were the personal issues of people and others have included state and national issues. I'm learning now that I can't spread myself so thin that I am only doing small surface level things with muliple people that remain strangers. Better I could plunge into one area of focus. I can help that section, praying for the Lord's provision and guidance to expand and help more. How great it is to plunge into true relationships? It is also hard. It's easy to say you love someone on the surface. It's very much harder when the more you learn about a person the things that you know as perfect goes away. Just like they say the honeymoon phase wears off in marriage. You will see the good, bad, and maybe the ugly. Not only will you see that about them. They will also see that about you. I would say that has been one of the hardest things I have learned as an adult. There is no such thing as a perfect mom, dad, or grandparent. Christ is the only perfect one!

The more you spend time with a person you will find that thing or quirk that will make you mad, bother you, or possibly make you reconsider the relationship all together. I have been ghosted[50]plenty of times but, I never ghost people. If you open up to others and their experiences think about that small thing that says, "Oh they won't get that." The judgment of others can slowly creep in if you aren't paying attention to the thoughts you are having.

"This person isn't smart."

"This person isn't able."

"This person is stagnant."

What does the Bible say about being judgemental?

"Do you suppose, O man—you who judge those who practice such things and yet do them yourself—that you will escape the judgment of God?" Romans 2:3 ESV[51]

"Do not judge by appearances, but judge with right judgement." John 7:24 ESV[52]

---

[50] "WHEN SOMEONE YOU TALK TO OFTEN SUDDENLY STOPS SPEAKING TO YOU AND IGNORES ALL YOUR MESSAGES." HTTPS://WWW.URBANDICTIONARY.COM/DEFINE.PHP?TERM=GHO STED

[51] https://www.bible.com/bible/59/ROM.2.3

[52] https://www.bible.com/bible/compare/JHN.7.24

"Why do you pass judgment on your brother? Or you, why do you despise your brother? For we will all stand before the judgment seat of God;" Romans 14:10 ESV[53]

We are not to be the judge of if someone decided to be lazy or become an overachiever. Maybe they were raised in a household where achieving isn't a goal. Maybe after a childhood of overachievement they are recovering in this season, taking a break. Only God knows the intricacies of another person's life and their true motivation. Something that drilled that home for me in my family is the barrage of questions my family would ask a person that started coming around more. Why didn't you go to school? Who is your mom? Why are you not close to your family? If I have learned nothing else from being in this crazy world of trauma recovery, it is that there is trauma in more of the majority of the populace than I thought. It makes me think about the individuals I meet so much more indepth. I was able to begin to let go of my unrealistic expectations in all of my relationships.

Trauma has been a major part of my life even unknowingly at times. For the majority of my life even pre-dating: my sexual assault which started my

53 https://www.bible.com/bible/59/rom.14.10

dive into trauma. When you begin to address your personal trauma or "severe mental or emotional stress or physical injury; an emotional upset; wound."[54] It gets messy, overwhelming, and exhausting fast. It helped me to begin to separate how God designed us versus how this broken world treats us and my emotions. Repeatedly, pointing to we have more work to do. "What?" This question itself shows our unbelief, our unwillingness to explore, our unwillingness to do the work, and our possible detached outlook at the world where everything we hear we block it out. More self work.

Many of my unrealistic expectations were in my dating relationships. I wanted access to my person at all times. The only excuses I accepted were the death of a family member or family emergency. Then at one point I thought about how much I hate talking on the phone. How I get into moods where I don't feel like talking but, I do it anyway. Why would I expect anyone to be there for me 24/7? On one hand, I knew from my past that people were never available for just you. On the other hand, I have been greatly aware now how much trauma others have been through. That caused me to be more gracious in my relationships. Some more than me, some less but,

---

[54] https://www.merriam-webster.com/dictionary/trauma

the more work I put into healing than worrying about my expectations of others. The more I see the people around me drowning in the expectations of others, their own expectations of themselves, and many other things people willingly signed up for, me included.

For instance, CHILDREN! Oh my gosh, I only have one. I could not imagine how people function with two, much less more. My daughter is six years old. After starting school at four, I not only had to deal with my emotions and her needs—I had to tackle with her the emotions carrying over from school. Be patient enough with her for her to tell me the issue. Arrange counselors to make sure that things that traumatized me didn't traumatize her. When starting school, the boys, friends, and bus drama was never ending. All while having to keep the house clean, get homework done, and keep me, her, the cat, and dog all spiritually, mentally, and physically well. I have begun to wonder why people get married and have more. That equals more trauma to work through and more places to fall short in my mind. I'm praying that God is healing families and marriages because I know that He is. It is amazing that any one of them ever last. Add in tons of social media, cultural pressure, church pressure, family pressure, in laws pressure, lack of morals in society, politcs, so on and so forth.

All a miracle of God that we can survive on this planet with the many expectations we place on ourselves. Then, the ones we place on others. As life goes on, we need more capacity to survive the thousands of side jobs we do, and our limits continue to decline. I was listening to Jennifer Rothschild's 4:13[55] podcast this morning and this topic was right on the nose. Her name is Crystal Paine author of "The Time Saving Mom." She said, "God made her with two hands, so she focuses on doing two things really well each day." Different things each day but only two. Everything else for the day the progress is satisfactory. I totally agree with her but, I hadn't made it to the specific number of two. I've found the same to be true. If I schedule more than two things in a day outside of my routine, I end up utterly depleted. For example, if I have two meetings on one day that is all my brain can handle. One needs to be in the morning and one in the afternoon, so I have time to prepare for the meeting, process the meeting, complete tasks related to the meeting, and get kind of squared away. Have lunch then repeat. By then it's time to go home, get the kid, clean, and bed.

It comes back full circle to expectations. Me letting go of my expectations of these people in my

[55] https://www.jenniferrothschild.com/stop-being-control-freak-mom-crystal-paine/

life, I thought it would release them. It actually released me. Released from the energy I was using to try to hold them to that standard. I was only able to do that with 15+ years of therapy. While learning more about God, connections, and the development of a person. It allowed me to forgive but not forget. I was slowly learning how to tread lightly and keep my heart protected. Where this became most evident for me is in my friendships. Usually, my internal dialogue was noticing my anger that no one was ever available in my greatest times of need. The most evident manifestation of this was with someone I love dearly. Simply like a stand in mom. What I felt like a mom should be:

- Return my phone calls
- Return my texts
- Listen to me when I speak
- WANT TO KNOW ME

Expectations when it came to my mom was a whole different ballgame. I learned that some of the things I expected were unfair to her. Only now can Isee that my mom was severely depressed and doing a lot more than she should have been. She still has things on her plate that she has been trying to get off for ten plus years. I'm just learning to take things off my own plate. I wanted a mom who was a mix between a stay at home mom and working mom. The mother God gave me was a working mother, a people serving mother, and a late education seeking mom. In the midst, of two crazily opposite kids going through school and a couple of marriages. It's a blessing that all of us are alive and mentally well.

Perfect dad, yeah, I don't think I ever expected that. Just because many men I've experienced make lots of mistakes unapologetically. My grandparents though are more perfect than I could ever ask them to be. They could be a little less selfless but, what would that change at 70 years old. They are the best. I realized some time in high school that my grandfather had two outside children. I knew though my grandparents had met in school and married at age 20. That took a little while for me to process and get over. My grandmother at the same time has loosened up her judgemental voice a lot in the past 20 years. They are perfect. Their lives of service overshadows all of that for me. That give me HOPE!

Pay attention now! Not just general H-O-P-E hope but HOPE IN CHRIST! It's the one, who intercedes on our behalf so we can be loved fully and thoroughly without works. Merriam-Webster defines hope as a "cherish a desire with anticipation; to want something to happen or to be true." What I like better are the synonyms: trust and reliance. We are called to trust and rely on Christ moment to moment. The more you learn about yourself and your story you will know why. Let's see how scripture talks about hope:

> "So that by two unchangeable things, in which it is impossible for God to lie, we who have fled for refuge might have strong encouragement to hold fast to the hope set before us. We have this as a sure and steadfast anchor of the soul, a hope that enters into the inner place behind the curtain, where Jesus has gone as a forerunner on our behalf, having become a high priest forever after the order of Melchizedek." Hebrews 6:18-20 ESV[56]

> "Therefore, since we have been justified by faith, we have peace with God through our Lord Jesus Christ. Through him we have also obtained access by faith into this grace in which we stand, and we rejoice in hope of the glory of God. Not only that, but we rejoice in our sufferings, knowing that suffering produces endurance, and endurance produces character, and character produces hope, and hope does not put us to shame,

---

[56] https://bible.com/bible/59/heb.6.18-20.ESV

because God's love has been poured into our hearts through the Holy Spirit who has been given to us." Romans 5:1-5 ESV[57]

"We who are strong have an obligation to bear with the failings of the weak, and not to please ourselves. Let each of us please his neighbor for his good, to build him up. For Christ did not please himself, but as it is written, "The reproaches of those who reproached you fell on me." For whatever was written in former days was written for our instruction, that through endurance and through the encouragement of the Scriptures we might have hope. May the God of endurance and encouragement grant you to live in such harmony with one another, in accord with Christ Jesus, that together you may with one voice glorify the God and Father of our Lord Jesus Christ. Therefore welcome one another as Christ has welcomed you, for the glory of God." Romans 15:1-7 ESV[58]

"Why are you cast down, O my soul, and why are you in turmoil within me? Hope in God;

[57] https://bible.com/bible/59/rom.5.1-5.ESV
[58] https://bible.com/bible/59/rom.15.2-6.ESV

for I shall again praise him, my salvation"
Psalm 42:5 ESV[59]

"The steadfast love of the Lord never ceases;
his mercies never come to an end; they are
new every morning; great is your faithfulness.
"The Lord is my portion," says my soul,
"therefore I will hope in him." Lamentations
3:22-24[60]

"I wait for the Lord, my soul waits, and in his
word, I hope;" Psalm 130:5[61]

Hope in Christ is all we have in this world of
despair. We turn on the news daily to see more
tragedies and things to be worried over. God though
wants our posture faced towards Him for the hope
He has already given us and the hope of things that
are to come. It's up to us to turn our eyes, hearts,
and mind to face His story of glory, hope, mercy, and
grace. He doesn't want us to be filled with despair
but with encouragement. In Christ, we see people
working together in the church, missions prospering
to help the community, and marriages flourishing to
bring honor to His name. Vastly different from what

---

[59] https://bible.com/bible/59/psa.42.5.ESV
[60] https://www.bible.com/bible/59/LAM.3.22-24
[61] https://www.bible.com/bible/59/PSA.130.5

we see im the world to give us hope for the perfect relationships we will find in heaven.

Trust

> "Blessed is the man who trusts in the Lord, whose trust is the Lord." Jeremiah 17:7[62]

> "Commit your way to the Lord; trust in him, and he will act." Psalm 37:5[63]

> "You keep him in perfect peace whose mind is stayed on you, because he trusts in you." Isaiah 26:3[64]

> "In you our fathers trusted; they trusted, and you delivered them." Psalm 22:4[65]

> "Trust in the Lord, and do good; dwell in the land and befriend faithfulness." Psalm 37:3[66]

> "I will say to the Lord, "My refuge and my fortress, my God, in whom I trust.""' Psalm 91:2[67]

Not only does God call us to hope, but He also calls us to trust Him. Just because you are following

---

[62] https://www.bible.com/bible/59/JER.17.7
[63] https://www.bible.com/bible/59/PSA.37.5
[64] https://www.bible.com/bible/59/ISA.26.3
[65] https://www.bible.com/bible/59/PSA.22.4
[66] https://www.bible.com/bible/59/PSA.37.3
[67] https://www.bible.com/bible/59/PSA.91.2

Christ it doesn't mean everything you want will go your way. Instead, God will begin to show you ways in which you can prioritize your life to be in line with His statutes. God calls us to trust that He has the ultimate plan for our lives not us. God knows the future. God created you. Why wouldn't you trust Him? He knew after sin was introduced to the world we would have anxieties. He gave us an avenue to release those burdens for Him to worry about not us. He just asks us to trust Him.

Faith

>""Behold, his soul is puffed up; it is not upright within him, but the righteous shall live by his faith." Habakkuk 2:4 ESV[68]

> "So then, those who are of faith are blessed along with Abraham, the man of faith." Galatians 3:9 ESV[69]

> "Since God is one—who will justify the circumcised by faith and the uncircumcised through faith." Romans 3:30 ESV[70]

---

[68] https://bible.com/bible/59/hab.2.4.ESV
[69] https://bible.com/bible/59/gal.3.9.ESV
[70] https://bible.com/bible/59/rom.3.30.ESV

> "Now faith is the assurance of things hoped for, the conviction of things not seen." Hebrews 11:1 ESV[71]

> "One Lord, one faith, one baptism," Ephesians 4:5 ESV[72]

Last but not least, we have to have faith. Faith in the fact that Christ will return. Faith that we all are the children of God. Faith that restoration is on the way for every single thing on this earth. In that restoration our relationship with God, Father, Holy Spirit, within ourselves, and within others will be made perfect.

---

[71] https://bible.com/bible/59/heb.11.1.ESV
[72] https://bible.com/bible/59/eph.4.5.ESV

Chapter Nine Direction:
Happiness vs. Joy

The world of before.......when I say before I don't mean before I found Christ as most say. I mean before the sun came up. I spent the majority of my life in what we would consider the storm, the dark cloud, or "the valley of the shadow of death[73]." Also different, I knew Christ while I was there. Not in the same way I do now but, I knew Him. Since, I had been suffering with depression since age 13 it's had been a large dark cloud over me with the exception of the last three years. Gratefully, I can see the sun again. God. Colors. Life. Joy.

The best way I can explain the experience of happiness is as a child you would enjoy pure excitement. You would come home daily ready to share with your parents the new thing I learned from the day. While in this I could see a child and remember being in that place but, I couldn't remember why I no longer had that excitement. When people described happy to me at that time, I would say I understood it to mean how you feel the moment you receive flowers. Instant happy feel of

---

[73] https://www.bible.com/bible/59/PSA.23.ESV

sorts, passing, not lasting at all. My happy turned into when things went my way. That may sound like something I could experience often but it was no more than once or twice a year. I came to learn it wasn't something I should expect or anticipate staying. My whole year looking towards two special days. Let me either smash your expectations or make you uncomfortable. Those days never were my birthday or Christmas.

My happiness became something I was looking for as opposed to something that was inside of me. As a boy crazy girl naturally, that came in the form of relationships. All other things aside as a child there are very few things you can control for yourself. What you wear, if you don't have uniforms. Who your friends are. What bookbag you want once a year if you are lucky. Quickly, possibly due to fairy tales, movies, or just something natural we begin to look for our mate. We want that one person with a mutual love that will be there through thick and thin even before knowing what that means. Adolescents outside of schoolwork is all about who likes who. From kindergarten through high school, I can remember who liked me and who didn't and list all of my crushes. All nonsense but how would I know to focus on anything different. Me being involved in the church early, you are around other believers, but kids have kid conversations. Adults have adult conversations. When are the adults involved in shaping the ideas of their children and when are children able to give the feedback that adults need to hear?

Me being able to listen helped me when it came to my daughter. Me listening to her not only fulfills my purpose, but it also prepares her for her's, and the gifts God has placed within her. She knows me and Christ are safe. She can always talk to us. Imagine what you can do with God in heaven on your side and one ally here on earth. It was always a priority for me to be a safe haven for everyone. That list included my friends, family members, kids, and clergy. It pulled back up for me the value learned from my family of don't forget the forgotten. Abuse magnified that for me. As early as the fourth grade, I had already been touched in appropriately by a trusted family member. I had no idea who to talk to about it. At that young, I didn't know how big the violation of trust was. I wasn't necessarily scared but, I was definitely confused. I held that information inside of myself until therapy helped me release it but, that one still affects me because I see this person quite regularly.

Verbal abuse came from the most unexpected sources and usually from someone I already liked enough to allow them to continue. Self worth was delayed for me for many reasons. Something to still work through but, I will say while still being involved with church hearing how much God loved me didn't help much when I felt hated by those close to me. When you are surrounded by evil it's hard to see the light, even when you don't recognize it yet. Nothing equips you to be the listener someone needs like going through the experience yourself. It's not that it equips you to say the right things but, it prevents you from saying the wrong things. I feel blessed to be that sanctuary for the women and men that I know have been abused and that I am especially equipped to remain open for my daughter. In that, I know it's my job to help those still living in abuse, pain, and suffering to see a glimmer of hope that is Christ. Years of being treated lowly it's not a far reach to see why I was mostly a pessemist.

Sex at one point became my happiness. While although, I knew it was a fleeting happiness to me it was better than no happiness at all. I felt wanted and cared for at least during that session. I could deal with the loneliness as it came. The climax of the change for me came when my daughter was conceived. This tied into my drinking as well. I planned for my night to go out with my cousin to have a few drinks and just hang out with him and his girlfriend. Before they made it to my house, I let a guy come over I had known for ten years or more. He was an exboyfriend I hadn't seen in a while. I thought well I am pretty safe since I am on the family compound. Someone would hear me if I screamed. Little did I know that night I would be sexually assaulted. I let my cousin know when he arrived and told him I would like to still go out to drink the night's events away. He let me. We partied the night away and I decided to call the boyfriend I had broken up with before Christmas. It was now January. When we were together, we were not being wise and was trying for a child. This night I went over before going home while drunk and I had told him about my perdicament. This drunken abused night led to the conception of my daughter.

My cycle was maybe one or two days late. No biggie at all but, I worked with my friends at the time. I decided to take a pregnancy test for jokes. The joke was on me because mommy life was swiftly on the way. I didn't tell any of my family except my mother, bonus mom, father, grandparents, and brothers along with a few cousins. I decided to inform my grandmother's siblings that Easter with an ultrasound picture in an envelope. I handed them the envelopes then sprinted outside to hang back with my cousins. I left them to discuss it because I knew there would be many opinions I didn't care to know.

Funny enough my favorites ended up being my worst critics. I won't specify but one said "I am disappointed in you." Imagine the story I just told you and that's the response you get. No benefit of the doubt. No questions. Nothing. I received a similar response from a different family member which I can't remember in its entirety. It summed up to "I thought you were smarter than that." Both caused enormous problems for me and those family members. One I was never close with again. The other it made us closer. I think the relationship that was made closer was accomplished through for the first time I did not hold my tongue. I said in the most respectful way I could that "you shouldn't have anything to say about my sex life if you didn't feel it necessary to come give me a sex talk before the age of 23." I was hurt because it put me back in a space, I had been my whole life. Unheard. Unseen. Just a problem.

This experience God put me through perfectly qualified me for the work I do on the ultrasound bus. I know what it feels like to be hit by a man, I know what it feels like to be alone, I know how it feels to be overwhelmed, and I know the turmoil in your head when you see that positive pregnancy test. All of this I can use to listen and be empathetic to any situation I come upon. I know that with one change in circumstance my life could be theirs and vice versa. Human to human relating through life experience. You don't need to have the same life experiences in order to be a listening ear and empathize with others.

All of these instances let to me being dragged further and further away from happiness. Yet, God brought me back through the kind hearts that surrounded me in my church. People who listened. People who helped pay for my counseling. People who didn't understand fully but tried. People who saw I was exhausted and at my end. People who saw beyond my circumstances to see my potential so much that they forced me to see it too. I saw biblical counselors and trauma counselors for the past four to five years. I have processed so much information without knowing how it was affecting my mind, body, and soul. It is amazing that I made it. A miracle I survived. A Jesus touched healing that my heart stayed tender. A blessing that my daughter has my heart. Many things I could say that reassures me Jesus put me back on His path to joy.

God's Joy

"A joyful heart is good medicine, but a crushed spirit dries up the bones." Proverbs 17:22 ESV[74]

> ""For you shall go out in joy and be led forth in peace; the mountains and the hills before you shall break forth into singing, and all the trees of the field shall clap their hands." Isaiah 55:12 ESV[75]

> "These things I have spoken to you, that my joy may be in you, and that your joy may be full." John 15:11 ESV[76]

> "For the kingdom of God is not a matter of eating and drinking but of righteousness and peace and joy in the Holy Spirit." Romans 14:17 ESV[77]

"I have no greater joy than to hear that my children are walking in the truth." 3 John 1:4 ESV[78]

Merriam Webster defines joy as, "to experience great pleasure or delight." Joy is an emotion of God

---

[74] https://bible.com/bible/59/pro.17.22.ESV
[75] https://bible.com/bible/59/isa.55.12.ESV
[76] https://bible.com/bible/59/jhn.15.11.ESV
[77] https://bible.com/bible/59/rom.14.17.ESV
[78] https://bible.com/bible/59/3jn.1.4.ESV

but it's not that simple. It's an emotion granted to us. He wants us to be enjoying life. He doesn't want us to live a life of fleeting happiness. Joy is something sustainable by staying connected to him. Intertwined with joy is the hope of something more. This is a hope that only Christ can give for more.

Chapter Ten Ministry Now!

My grandmother a woman who never missed putting flowers on the graves of family members including a child of her own. She always welcomed extended family to share a meal. All inclusive of family spouses, girlfriends, boyfriends, kid's friends, new pastors and their families. She would never turn down serving a meal to neighborhood kids. My grandparents are the ones who rose to the occasion and poised the kids of the community to pick up trash for miles to teach us the importance of the upkeep of the community. A good while before it was formally taught in schools. You would think a couple of times before tossing that piece of paper out of the bus window. It would be there waiting on you the next summer.

My grandfather was a firefighter chief. I haven't talked to him much about this yet, but it's been heavy on my heart lately. Do we live our lives in a way where we are looking at our job anticipating needs? Are we thoroughly seeking our community as an opportunity to instill values for the future? Are we seeing things that should happen at church and just taking that initiative to complete the task? Are we running the torch of hope to the people in need, to the sick and to the people that are hurting? What I mean by that is being a fire chief wasn't his primary profession. It was his job after his nine to five. He drove dump trucks during the day hauling various materials. Then, served our local community fire station and trained them to put out fires and help the community. They didn't just fight fires though. Out of that building: elections were held, summer lunches were served, and summer lessons were taught. He volunteered for them all. The building began to be used for baby showers, small parties, and even some big memorable ones. The trash pickup began to be something they helped with. From that one little building in our community, lives and houses were saved, a playground and meeting area came to being, and a storm shelter for the protection of others sprouted. Through those actions of a few they built what it means for me now to be a community.

Do we take advantage of those same moments? Not looking to be recognized but to just take initiative because it's my community. For example, when you leave a public restroom do you turn around and ensure you left it clean? When you wash your hands, do you use that napkin to wipe the counter in front of you? Its interesting this chapter topic is coming at this exact time. I decided why am I waiting for the church to be ready when I've alread saw it myself and determined there is a need. After seeing the need, God gave me a thought. The timing was off from the church dynamics at the time. I was stumped and stopped in my tracks. After many days of wrestling and praying, I felt that slap in the forehead DUH moment. You have the whole ministry you started and aren't using DUH DUH DUH! At that moment, everything came together. All we need is Christ alone to serve God to spread love in the world. A person having other people to support them and join in your fight is just a plus. Even if no one gets on board YOUR ministry is still needed HERE NOW AND IN YOUR COMMUNITY!

It doesn't have to be a business. It doesn't have to have an official: name, website or plan. Christ alone is enough! He can use you exactly how you are, scars and all. Mistakes and all to touch the lives of others. Your smile could be your ministry. Your goal everyday could be to share that smile with every person you run across that day. Imagine what could change about your community.

In Everyday Life

Let's back up to November 2021. I fell down the four concrete steps on my back porch. Me thinking I sprained something I thought I would jump up and limp into the house. What actually happened was in my attempt to rise I lost my lunch. I thought "oh this isn't good." Long story short, after syndesmosis[79] surgery and a chipped bone at the bottom of my leg I ended up in a wheelchair and boot for six weeks. I had not even a month prior moved into this new home 45 minutes away from my hometown at the request of my church family. The very same day my grandmother was being released from the hospital post back surgery and a stroke. I was disappointed in myself because now I could not help. I added the burden to someone of my five year old daughter. I felt horrible.

My grandparents had every single day of my life on this earth sacrificed for me to have, do, exist, be, and grow. When something was wrong, I was supposed to swoop in to help. It was not for a pat on the back but, I wanted to show my deep appreciation of every sacrifice they made for me. I talked to them everyday, sometimes multiple times a day. I also called during this period to keep up with all the updates. I kept apologizing over and over that I couldn't help and, I was so sorry. Also, that I loved them. My grandfather said, "That is why you do all you can every single day. When you can't you've

---

[79] where your two leg bones are pulled apart from each other

already given your all and shown your love, not waiting for the end to do it." A feeling of relief rushed over me. I was thinking back over their aging years, my grandparents have been retired since I was born or close to it. They have used every waking moment to serve others. They gave their all before their bodies betrayed them. Even now they still go out of their way to do things for others and rarely do things for themselves. They did the work. Now they can enjoy their rest and what God has for them while they are not able to go as they could before.

A funny thing I've noticed about myself recently is that I am messy. My small acts of let me sit this here could turn into a home for this placed item. I sit at a certain desk to do my nine to five work. It is right beside my couch. Everything I want to clear off my desk between that time gets placed on this area of my couch. The logical next step would be to put up everthing back in its home but. . . Instead, I move right onto the next task to be done. On and on until I reach that level of intolerance to where the whole house has to be cleaned in one go. Me noticing this about myself allowed me to be a better parent about my daughter's cleaning ability. I was able to extend grace to her and show her things in small increments to better both of our lives. It allowed me to relate to her and learn about us both.

In My Community

I worked at a retail pharmacy for five years. When I started, I had no retail experience. One time I ran across an article on the internet, I decided to use in my new role as a cashier was to compliment one thing about every customer who came through my checkout line. When I moved to the beauty counter it was something I could build from because I was sought out for, trusted with advice on the appearance of my customer. That one thing bridged the gap to a relationship with my local community. It changed my outlook on the job. I started studying the weekly advertisements to help my customers save money. If during checkout, I saw something that had a coupon I scanned it, if there was a buy one get one free or buy one get one 50% off sale, I would tell them and sometimes they wouldn't even know I scanned it on their behalf. It didn't matter if they knew, it was about a small act of kindness. You never know where people need to stretch that dollar to. I give God Almighty the credit for giving me that insight so young. He gave me a ministry in my day to day job when I showed up for work. I began to love it. The mission is always the same: LOVE OTHERS AND LOVE GOD.

"Jesus answered, "The most important is, 'Hear, O Israel: The Lord our God, the Lord is one. And you shall love the Lord your God with all your heart and with all your soul and with all your mind and with all your strength.' The second is this: 'You shall love your neighbor as yourself.' There is no other commandment greater than these."" Mark 12: -31[80]

There are many different ways to show that love. Through God, acts of kindness, acts of service, donating, and even just a smile. We've explored prayer and service. Let me think back to some other things I've seen. The show 'Undercover Boss' changed my life. It was the reason I was able to keep myself encouraged at my pharmacy job. I would tell myself at any moment someone could walk in here and think I deserved to be in a higher position than I was. God is an expert a flipping the script. Remember: "But many who are first will be last, and the last first." Matthew 19:30 ESV[81]

He brings it around full circle. Have you ever heard a celebrity say, "you see the same people on the way up as you see on the way down." Even

[80] https://www.bible.com/bible/59/MRK.12.29-31
[81] https://bible.com/bible/59/mat.19.30.ESV

though we get that advice do we live our lives out any differently? The first time I considered myself grateful for having a caring heart was when my daughter started preschool. I wanted to be far away from my hometown. Let me tell you something I learned about God. He will sit you back in the same spot as many times as He needs in order for you to learn the lesson.

Here I was in my hometown, at a job I hated but wanted to love. It was made hard by a number of things. I had the degrees. I received my master's the first year of her life. I can tell you confidently degrees don't mean squat if you don't have a job to use it in. I had business ideas but no money to market it. I could have gone door to door but, being introverted paralyzed my actions. I realized Arpi would go to school in a place where everyone knew me and expected a lot of me. I still ended up in the same crab bucket as them. Us trying to claw our way out. I knew there would be substitute teachers here that knew me and if their memory of me wasn't pleasant my daughter would suffer the consequences. That sobered me quickly to my past and made me glad that wasn't something I would need to worry myself with because even in my youth I tried to love all.

This played out in a much more practical way one time recently, I was at my wits end and frustrated because my car that was given to me free of charge two years prior was giving me tons of anxiety. Not that it didn't happen before with the other car but, now it was more important because I had a child. I know what it felt like to be teased because of the car you drove, the clothes you wore, and what your mom looked like. This although in the back of my mind was not my main concern. My daughter had a doctor's appointment about an hour and a half away. It was important and I needed to make it happen. Why did I? Not sure?.........schedule this on a Sunday. I thought it would be less busy and quick. I reserved a rental car. The munchkin was in the car sleep with the windows down. We had just left church and with her being sleep it would be a quick in and out. I walked through the door, heard people talking on cell phones, the business phone ringing off the hook, and at least ten people in this small office. I stood patiently waiting on my turn as I saw the lady beside me get upset because she seemed to have gotten in a wreck and they had no cars available until Tuesday, among other setbacks. I kept hearing nothing available, nothing available, nothing available while I was looking out the window making sure the munchkin was still sleep.

While people watching as I always do I see someone I know. A girl I went to school with previously in middle school. So long ago, I didn't think she remembered me so I kept people watching. Then I heard, "You can come on up Bree." When I heard Bree, I knew she remembered me because I've always gone by my middle name. Only in places of business would I hear Ms. Alloway or "X-avia." I walk up to the counter. She says "I have you all set. Swipe here for your $300 deposit. I will park in the front and be out shortly." How great is our God that He puts a ram in the bush to provide for our needs. To love His impatient child Bree so dearly to get her out of a room where she was having sensory overload. To have a car available just for me. I asked for a mid sized car. I am overweight and small cars make me claustrophobic. She upgraded me to a Nissan Juke at the same price as the car and I was out of there. If I would have been mean to her in school, would she have skipped me in the line to get me out quicker? Would she have told me my car was unavailable and given it to someone else? Would she have upgraded my vehicle? Would she have had one relaxed transaction in the sea of that mess of people in that office? We were able to be a blessing to each other in that moment. A moment that could have easily been used by the devil. Used for OUR good. Not just only mine.

Every time something that even seemingly small happens, I am so assured that God loves me a little more. Thank you, Holy Spirit! Every time no matter how many times He does this a day, week, or month it feels brand new. I'm as shocked as the first time it ever happened. These are reminders that you are not alone. God sees and He cares. I feel so blessed to live in a family that we knew as second nature to treat others how we would treat all family. Even in elementary school I can remember talking with the janitors and just having those sweet relationships surrounding my life.

Only when you are out exploring the world do you know things to be different. Not every household was raised to say yes ma'ams and no sirs. We had residential assistants, RAs similar to college to keep us in line from time to time so it was frowned upon to call a 20-25 year old a ma'am or sir. They were in the prime of their lives. They didn't want to know any different. After adapting to that bunch, I moved to Louisiana for college where although we were still in the south the ma'ams and sirs were appreciated but pre-50 you may only want to keep it contained to your brain only. Showing by just a common courtesy of respect because they didn't want to seem a bit old even in their 60s and 70s. I would call Louisiana the land of the youth because they know how to relax and enjoy life. I never seen someone take a weekend so serious until I landed there. Ask a girl that has lived and been raised in the south, that was a habit to break after so much training to say it. It all comes back to valuing a life. One person as an individual person to person. Ma'am and Sir is the south's way of acknowledging I know you have some wisdom that I don't yet contain, and I will follow your instruction because I respect that.

Although some members of my family seem to have majority good or bad traits. The truth is each person I've mentioned has both. That means they will bring someone joy and they will disappoint someone. We all will. God though provides us with the relationship we long for our whole lives. A relationship of total acceptance and love. No one can be more perfectly fitted to love you than your creator.

"Before I formed you in the womb I knew you, and before you were born I consecrated[82]you;

---

[82] Oxford English Dictionary defines concecrated as "being made or declared; declared to be or represent the body and blood of Christ." https://www.oed.com/dictionary/consecrated_adj?tl=true

I appointed you a prophet to the nations."
Jeremiah 1:5[83]

There are characteristics good and bad that we take from our families, blood or chosen. Regardless, we are called to return to our true family in Christ which is where we belong, not in our families of origin. Now you were intentionally placed there to form your traits, tendencies, and tenderness. It's up to you to keep what's important and to discard the rest.

The books that helped me tremendously in these last three years of constant growth were:

- "Psalms 23: The Shepherd with Me" by Jennifer Rothschild[84]
- "A Shepherd Looks at Psalms 23" by W. Phillip Keller[85]
- "Because He Loves Me" by Elyse Fitzpatrick[86]

---

[83] https://www.bible.com/bible/59/JER.1.5

[84] Rothschild, Jennifer. Psalm 23: The Shepherd with Me. Lifeway. 2018. Brentwood.

[85] Keller, W. Phillip. A Shepherd Looks at Psalms 23. Zondervan. 2007. Grand Rapids.

[86] Fitzpatrick, Elyse. Because He Loves Me. Crossway. 2010. Wheaton.

o "Found in Him: The Joy of the Incarnation and Our Union with Christ"by Elyse Fitzpatrick[87]

They each in their own way awakened me to how personal God truly is. Me looking back now I would probably say I thought Jesus was personal, God was distant but still cared, and the Holy Spirit was waiting and anticipating a gathering. Jesus was the only hands on one that cared about my day-to-day life. Now I know that's not true but, I believed that while still being a devoted believer, and studying God's Word daily. I know what it feels like to be reading God's Word and pastors saying you are missing something. "No, I got it. I read it. I understand." There is a reason in Joshua 1:8 it states,

> "This Book of the Law shall not depart from your mouth, but you shall meditate on it day and night, so that you may be careful to do according to all that is written in it. For then you will make your way prosperous, and then you will have good success." Joshua 1:8 ESV[88]

Not just to read the Word but meditate on it. Meditation in Greek is "meletao" or "melete" to "care for," "to attend to," "to be diligent in." In

---

[87] Fitzpatrick, Elyse. Found in Him: The Joy of the Incarnation and Our Union with Christ. Crossway. 2013. Wheaton.
[88] https://bible.com/bible/59/jos.1.8.ESV

Hebrew "hawgaw" or "to murmur or ponder." It's an immersive act that you get something from other than comprehension. Think about the phrase "Jesus loves me." How many times have you heard it from birth to now, even if not from a religious family. People passing out freebies saying Jesus loves you, shirts, billboards, car tags, the list goes on. Just by seeing those words does that make you believe them? No, probably not. Similar to meeting someone new and as soon as you meet, they say:

"I love you"

Possible responses:

> "What?"

> "You don't know me."

> "I don't know you."

> "Prove it."

> "You haven't done anything for me."

> "I haven't done anything for you."

Let's talk about your automatic responses.

Response one: "Are you talking to the right person?"

God's Response:

"For whenever our heart condemns us, God is greater than our heart, and he knows everything." 1 John 3:20 ESV[89]

He knows all.

"That this is God, our God forever and ever. He will guide us forever." Psalm 48:14 ESV[90]

He guides us. He knows who He guides.

"O Lord, you have searched me and known me! You know when I sit down and when I rise up; you discern my thoughts from afar. You search out my path and my lying down and are acquainted with all my ways. Even before a word is on my tongue, behold, O Lord, you know it altogether." Psalm 139:1-4 ESV[91]

He knows our thoughts and our paths, present, past, and future.

"The Lord our God be with us, as he was with our fathers. May he not leave us or forsake us," 1 Kings 8:57 ESV[92]

He is always with us.

Response Two: "You don't know me."

---

[89] https://bible.com/bible/59/1jn.3.20.ESV
[90] https://bible.com/bible/59/psa.48.14.ESV
[91] https://bible.com/bible/59/psa.139.1-4.ESV
[92] https://bible.com/bible/59/1ki.8.57.ESV

God's Response:

> "Therefore, knowing the fear of the Lord, we persuade others. But what we are is known to God, and I hope it is known also to your conscience." 2 Corinthians 5:11 ESV[93]

We are known to God. He knows us intimately not with a long arm stick or through someone else.

> "Your eyes saw my unformed substance; in your book were written, every one of them, the days that were formed for me, when as yet there was none of them." Psalm 139:16 ESV[94]

He created us. How could He not know us? He took the time to give us His traits.

Response Three: "Prove it."

God's Response:

> "The God who equipped me with strength and made my way blameless." Psalm 18:32 ESV[95]

[93] https://bible.com/bible/59/2co.5.11.ESV
[94] https://bible.com/bible/59/psa.139.16.ESV
[95] https://bible.com/bible/59/psa.18.32.ESV

He strengthens us in hard times. He sent Jesus so we could have a more intimate relationship with Him.

> "For this time, I will send all my plagues on you yourself, and on your servants and your people, so that you may know that there is none like me in all the earth." Exodus 9:14 ESV[96]

He makes it known He is the most powerful and the creator of the Earth.

> "So, God created man in his own image, in the image of God he created him; male and female he created them." Genesis 1:27 ESV[97]

He wanted us to look like Him as we would like for our kids to resemble us.

> "And the angel answered her, "The Holy Spirit will come upon you, and the power of the Most High will overshadow you; therefore the child to be born will be called holy—the Son of God." Luke 1:35 ESV[98]

He sent Jesus, His son for us to be rescued.

---

[96] https://bible.com/bible/59/exo.9.14.ESV
[97] https://bible.com/bible/59/gen.1.27.ESV
[98] https://bible.com/bible/59/luk.1.35.ESV

"And Jesus uttered a loud cry and breathed his last. And the curtain of the temple was torn in two, from top to bottom. And when the centurion, who stood facing him, saw that in this way he breathed his last, he said, "Truly this man was the Son of God!"" Mark 15:37-39 ESV[99]

Jesus sent by God, died for us to prove God is God and Son is Son. Also, that They are one.

Response four: "You haven't done anything for me."

God's Response:

"Come and see what God has done: he is awesome in his deeds toward the children of man." Psalm 66:5 ESV[100]

He forgives and is lenient on us when we should be smote[101].

"It has seemed good to me to show the signs and wonders that the Most High God has done for me." Daniel 4:2 ESV[102]

---

[99] https://bible.com/bible/59/mrk.15.37-39.ESV
[100] https://bible.com/bible/59/psa.66.5.ESV
[101] Killed instantly for sin
[102] https://bible.com/bible/59/dan.4.2.ESV

He cares about our faith. He constantly assures us that He is present.

> "For God has done what the law, weakened by the flesh, could not do. By sending his own Son in the likeness of sinful flesh and for sin, he condemned sin in the flesh," Romans 8:3 ESV[103]

God sent His Son to pay for our sins so that we could have His perfect record and commune with God.

> "More than that, we also rejoice in God through our Lord Jesus Christ, through whom we have now received reconciliation." Romans 5:11 ESV[104]

It is because of Jesus we can have fellowship with God. Our sin is now atoned for and satisfied.

> "The Lord has done what he purposed; he has carried out his word, which he commanded long ago; he has thrown down without pity; he has made the enemy rejoice over you and exalted the might of your foes." Lamentations 2:17 ESV[105]

---

[103] https://bible.com/bible/59/rom.8.3.ESV
[104] https://bible.com/bible/59/rom.5.11.ESV
[105] https://bible.com/bible/59/lam.2.17.ESV

God is true to what He says. That makes Him trustworthy.

> "And you have seen all that the Lord your God has done to all these nations for your sake, for it is the Lord your God who has fought for you." Joshua 23:3 ESV[106]

God fights for us in all circumstances.

> "The Lord is my shepherd; I shall not want. He makes me lie down in green pastures. He leads me beside still waters. He restores my soul. He leads me in paths of righteousness for his name's sake. Even though I walk through the valley of the shadow of death, I will fear no evil, for you are with me; your rod and your staff, they comfort me. You prepare a table before me in the presence of my enemies; you anoint my head with oil; my cup overflows. Surely goodness and mercy shall follow me all the days of my life, and I shall dwell in the house of the Lord forever." Psalm 23:1-6 ESV[107]

He is our shepherd that is with us from fertilization to dust. Faithful.

---

[106] https://bible.com/bible/59/jos.23.3.ESV
[107] https://bible.com/bible/59/psa.23.1-6.ESV

Returing to your responses to the fact that Jesus loves you:

1. "What?"

This question implies a couple of things. One, you don't know who Jesus is if your first response is what. A possibility not a guarantee. You may know His name but, not His nature or character. Possibly today is your first time being exposed to the name Jesus. If so, we have some learning to do. All of that is okay but, it still speaks to how we are interpreting the message.

Two, love! It is a possibility that you don't know what love is. Hint hint, which probably means the same thing, you don't know Jesus and His character. Or you could have a similar experience to me and knew what love was then life muddled it all up with the lying, perversions, and abuse of people.

2. "I don't know you."

I am going to leave that one right here. Refer to number one.

3. "I haven't done anything for you to love me." Another I problem. God doesn't expect us to do anything but, to accept His love. The thing we have to do to accept Him, is to learn more about Him and pay attention to His work in our lives. Me learning

about the work of God, Jesus Christ, and the Holy Spirit allowed me to free myself from the expectations and allowed me to live in peace as God designed and created me to be. He doesn't want me rushing through my day, being overly productive, reaching to achieve that next goal and not enjoying life, listening, and learning from Him while at the same time getting a chance to serve Him by showing His love to others. What a blessing to be able to release all expectations to do what God puts on your plate today while He provides for you, protects you, and loves you. A birth to death love affair for the ages. I am praying for you on your journey to purpose and see you next time. . .

Made in the USA
Columbia, SC
01 March 2025

54563511R00090